The *Christmas* BOOK

A Treasury of the Sights, Sounds, Crafts, Tastes & Joys of the Season

ORTHO BOOKS

Ortho Books

Publisher
Robert J. Dolezal

Production Director
Ernie S. Tasaki

Managing Editors
Karin Shakery
Michael D. Smith
Sally W. Smith

System Manager
Leonard D. Grotta

National Sales Manager
Charles H. Aydelotte

Marketing Specialist
Susan B. Boyle

Operations Coordinator
Georgiann Wright

Administrative Assistant
Deborah Tibbetts

Senior Technical Analyst
J. A. Crozier, Jr.

Address all inquiries to
Ortho Books
Chevron Chemical Company
Consumer Products Division
Box 5047
San Ramon, CA 94583

Copyright © 1987
Chevron Chemical Company
All rights reserved under international and Pan-American copyright conventions.

2 3 4 5 6 7 8 9
88 89 90 91 92

ISBN 0-89721-094-8
Library of Congress Catalog Card
Number 87-070188

Chevron Chemical Company
6001 Bollinger Canyon Road, San Ramon, CA 94583

ADDITIONAL WRITER
Judith Dunham

CONSULTANTS
Rebecca Baker Bradley and
Robert Noble
Bradley & Noble, San Francisco

Sharon M. Burke
California Christmas Tree Growers
Lafayette, Calif.

Pat Churchfield
Mill Valley, Calif.

Steve Gustafson
Silvestri Corp., San Francisco

Alisa A. de Jong-Stout, AIFD
El Cerrito, Calif.

Patric Powell
Bloomers, San Francisco

Si Spiegel
Hudson Valley Tree, Newburgh, NY

David Turner and John Martin
Turner-Martin, San Mateo, Calif.

Randall Whitehead
Light Source, San Francisco

Judie Worley
Orchard Nursery, Lafayette, Calif.

COPY CHIEF
Melinda Levine

COPYEDITORS
Andrea Connolly
Judith Dunham

EDITORIAL ASSISTANT
Tamara Mallory

EDITORIAL COORDINATOR
Kate Rider

ILLUSTRATORS
Edith Allgood: 160, 165
Max Seabaugh, MAX: 169

PHOTOGRAPHIC RESEARCHERS
Kate O'Keeffe
Deborah Parker
Pam Peirce

PHOTOGRAPHIC STYLISTS
Kate Pacoe: (for Laurie Black photos)
Sara Slavin: 81, 107, 109, 149,
    150 (above), 151, 154 (above),
    160, 161, 162, 164, 187 (above)

COMPOSITOR
Bob Miller

PRODUCTION COORDINATOR
Lezlly Freier

COLOR SEPARATOR AND LITHOGRAPHER
W. A. Krueger Company

Additional contributors on page 190

PHOTOGRAPHERS
Laurie Black
Douglas Manchee

ADDITIONAL PHOTOGRAPHERS
Bill Apton: 140 (above)
Lee Boltin: 13 (below), 15 (below)
Karen Bussolini, 156
Patricia Brabant: 144–145
Clyde Childress: 115
Alan Copeland: Front cover, 4, 21
    (above), 26, 133 (below)
Dr. Michael Dirr: 34, 35
Christine Douglas: 63, 117 (below)
Barbara Feigles: 9, 18, 19, 168
Mark E. Gibson: 6–7, 11, 45,
    133 (above)
John Hargett: 60
Saxon Holt: 8, 12
Roy Inman: 21 (below), 99
Ben Janken: 89
James H. Karales: 17, 20, 24,
    30 (below), 71 (above)
Kathryn Kleinman: 81, 107, 109,
    154 (above)
Susan Lammers: 116, 130
Michael Lamotte: 148, 149, 150,
    151, 161, 162, 164, 187
Fred Lyon: 112 (below)
Bruce Mathews: 31, 131
Jonathan A. Meyers: 10, 28,
    64 (below), 70, 132, 139
Pam Peirce: 32, 33, 36, 37, 38
Susan Roth: 22–23, 25
Barry Shapiro: 43
Nantee Smith: 157 (below)
Tom Tracy: 141 (above), 184, 185,
    186, 188
Jackson Vereen: 147, 148, 158, 159
Jessie Walker: 91 (below), 92,
    100–101, 119 (below), 125, 127

PHOTOGRAPHIC RESOURCES
Museum of Fine Arts, Houston,
    The Bayou Bend Collection,
    Gifts of Miss Ima Hogg: 80,
    102, 104 (above), 105, 128
Bettman Archives: 14, 29, 95, 163,
    171, 172 (above)
Callanwolde Fine Arts Center: 60
Charleston Trident Convention and
    Visitors Bureau: 30 (above)
Concord Museum, Concord, Mass.:
    103 (above), 157 (below)
Dover Archives: 27
Evergreen Press: 173 (left)
Gallier House, Tulane University:
    16, 103 (below)
Hallmark Cards: 180, 181, 182, 183
Gabriel Moulin Studios: 52
Oak Alley Plantation: 46, 47
Smith & Hawkin, Ltd.: 86
Southern Accents: 46–47

The Christmas BOOK

Created and designed by the editorial staff of Ortho Books

PROJECT EDITOR
Karin Shakery

DESIGNER
Laura Lamar

WRITERS
Alvin Horton
Karin Shakery

LAYOUT EDITOR
Linda Bouchard

CONTENTS

CHAPTER 1

Joy To The World

Rejoice and celebrate age-old traditions and customs of Christmas

For most Americans, Christmas centers around the home, where ties with family and friends are affirmed by joyful seasonal celebrations and rituals. This spirit of goodwill is the mood captured in the chapters of our book.

Joy to the World contains a brief history of the holiday—a celebration that originated long before the birth of Christ. It is followed by The Trees of Winter with information about how to select trees, keep them fresh, and make them safe. Baubles, Bangles & Beads sparkles with a host of exciting ideas for trees and ornaments and Deck the Halls is aglow with wreaths, garlands, and swags to hang inside or outside your home. The Magic of Light combines decorating ideas with specific technical information. The Treats of Christmas offers food for thought—decorative thought for table settings, garnishes, and cookies to hang on the tree. An explanation of how Santa came to play such a vital role in our celebrations can be found in The Giving of Gifts chapter along with ideas for thoughtful gifts and ways to wrap them.

Our aim is to present a book that will enable you and your family to enjoy a happy, joyful, decorative holiday this year and in the years to come. Merry Christmas.

Three very diverse but instantly recognizable symbols of Christmas are the church, preceding pages, the red bracts of a poinsettia, left, and a wreath on a window, right.

Christmas Past

The celebration of Christmas has assimilated practices that originated over many centuries and a wide geographical area. Many early customs were accepted by the Church during its history, enabling formerly pagan peoples to retain their familiar rituals by modifying them to serve Christian purposes.

Even the most secular observers of Christmas today have preserved many of the old practices, because of emotional ties that lingered after they broke with the religions of their childhood, or because the practices satisfy deep, universal human needs.

Winter Solstice Celebrations

Many familiar Christmas practices originated in prehistoric and early historic observances of the winter solstice, which occurs three or four days before December 25. Before the advent of modern conveniences that insulated people from the rigors and deprivations of winter, this shortest day of the year fell at the onset of the long, cold season of gloom and hardship. Yet the winter solstice also marked that point at which days began to lengthen and nights to shorten.

Not surprisingly, the key element in celebrations of the winter solstice was fire—the earthly manifestation of the sun, which is the source of light, warmth, and life-giving energy. Bonfires, hearth fires, and burning candles and lanterns were features central to recognizing the solstice. Many festivities incorporated evergreens such as holly, mistletoe, and ivy, which, by remaining evergreen, defied the winter and therefore promised the return of the sun.

Because supplies of fodder were often insufficient to sustain livestock through the winter, some of the domestic animals had to be slaughtered around the time of the solstice. This surfeit was used for feasting at the start of this lean season.

With the sudden bounty and the need to curry favor of sun gods and other deities of light and life—combined with the basic human desire to lighten periods of oppressiveness—solstice celebrations developed among many cultures. It was only natural that people wanted to gather close to the fire in houses decked with evergreens, toast each other, feast, sing, appease their gods, and look hopefully toward better—and longer—days.

Vikings celebrated the solstice as Yuletide, which included rites to insure good crops. They burned Yule logs, lighted with fire carefully kept from logs of the previous year. This custom had close parallels in southern Europe, in France, England, the Slavic countries, and Greece. Druids kindled fire using magic crystals and sunlight, and their people kissed beneath the sacred mistletoe. This evergreen, a symbol of goodwill and love, was an omen of long life, fertility, and happiness for those who kissed beneath it. Called allheal, mistletoe was finally accepted by the Church, which was quick to proclaim it a symbol of Christ, the Divine Healer.

Persians built fires on December 25 to worship their god of light, Mithras, by paying tribute to the birth of the Unconquered Sun. Egyptians honored Isis, mother of their sun god, Horus. In this season Jews lighted candles to celebrate Hanukkah, known as the Feast of Lights. Hanukkah is not a solstice celebration in itself, but it is nevertheless a custom using fire and held at the time of the solstice.

For a week in mid-December, ancient Romans revered Saturnalia with feasting, revelry, gift-giving, lighting of candles, decorating with berries and evergreens, a moratorium on war and personal enmity, and reversal of ranks and suspension of many workaday restrictions.

Above: According to legend, holly repels witches, lightning, and poison. Today the red berries are synonymous with Christmas decoration.
Opposite page: Fire played a very important role in the celebration of the winter solstice. The hearth is still a natural gathering place during winter festivities.

During this time, for instance, masters waited on their servants. Aspects of these practices, called misrule, have survived to this day in certain parts of England.

Close on the heels of the Saturnalia came the Calends. This Roman celebration of the New Year included feasting and revelry, the decoration of houses with greens, and the exchange of presents with wishes for prosperity and happiness in the coming year.

Because the date of the birth of Christ had long been argued by Christians, without coming to any consensus, the Church finally designated it in late December. It is not surprising that the birthday of the Bringer of Light and everlasting life should be celebrated close to the winter solstice.

The Middle Ages

By the advent of the Middle Ages in Europe, Christmas was becoming established as a great sacred holiday. St. Patrick brought it to Ireland, St. Augustine of Canterbury was soon to introduce it to England, and other monks took it to the countries of northern, central, and western Europe, and to the Slavic lands. The twelfth to the sixteenth centuries were the peak of joyous celebration in homes as well as churches. Masses glorified the birth of Christ, as did feasting, dancing, and carousing. Carols were sung, but the early ones, which tended toward bawdiness, were not condoned by the Church. Burlesques of Church liturgy were popular, and misrule, a legacy of the Calends, held sway. A carnival atmosphere surrounded various kinds of public celebration and mummery. Masques, or short allegorical performances, and other entertainments

were presented in the courts of medieval English kings, accompanied by huge feasts and the burning of great logs. In the reign of Edward IV of England, thousands of the poor were fed. The spirit and many practices of the ancient solstice celebrations survived and prevailed.

The Church tempered these revelries and further Christianized the celebrations of early winter by initiating mystery plays. In those times of pervasive illiteracy, mystery plays taught the laity the New Testament by dramatizing episodes from the life of Christ, often using some of the trappings of ancient non-Christian celebrations. The modern Christmas tree originated in one of these plays. The Church also decided to emphasize special days from Advent (the period beginning four Sundays before Christmas) to Epiphany (January 6). The saints' days falling in this period were given greater significance. These efforts of the Church competed with secular celebrations

A young child learns the meaning of Christmas by opening one door of an Advent calendar each day.

but ultimately further assimilated and Christianized them.

Many Christian legends that exist today began in the Middle Ages. For instance, it was said that, on Christmas at the stroke of midnight, animals could talk, and that a spirit of peace and adoration of the newborn Christ child pervaded all of nature, over all of the world. A related legend held that on the holiest of nights trees bowed and through the night birds sang their sweetest songs.

According to another legend, each year the Virgin Mary chose angels from heaven to wake small children and take them to Paradise to sing a

given to families, nursing and convalescent homes, and hospitals in the local area.

Fire departments in many cities gather toys for needy families who apply for assistance. And some firefighters volunteer to go to shopping centers and other public locations to collect items. People may also take donations directly to their local firehouse.

The police department is another municipal organization that may have an already established method for collecting, receiving, and distributing toys and food. Sometimes organizations prefer cash donations because they have made arrangements with particular manufacturers to purchase items at a discount.

The Salvation Army, an international organization with centers in eighty countries and in thousands of communities across the United States, is well known for its Christmas kettles, which are used to collect cash donations from holiday shoppers. Other Christmas programs sponsored by the Salvation Army include providing meals for homeless people, senior citizens in need, and shut-ins who are unable to cook for themselves. As part of the toy program in some cities, the Salvation Army sets up Christmas trees in shopping centers or other locations so that holiday shoppers can donate food and toys. In several communities the Salvation Army attaches small tags to the tree, each of which bears the description of a person, usually a child, who needs a gift. Shoppers select tags, take them on their errands, and return with gifts to which the tags are then attached before being placed under the tree.

It is not difficult to find a way to give to others at the Christmas holidays—whether through a community organization, your place of business, or your church. Over the years you and your family have probably developed your own way of celebrating Christmas. The joy of sharing with others can add meaning to your personal traditions.

Christmas is coming, the geese are getting fat,

Please put a penny in the old man's hat;

If you haven't got a penny, a ha'penny will do,

If you haven't got a ha'penny, God bless you!

Public displays of lit trees and tableaux can be enjoyed by all who pass by. They are often donated by corporations.

Fun and Games

O h what fun it is to ride on a one-horse open sleigh. . . ." "Here we come a wassailing among the leaves so green. . . ." "I'm dreaming of a white Christmas. . . ." So many of the traditional songs and carols sung at Christmastime are about the joy of celebrating the holidays amid falling snow and having fun in a "winter wonderland."

With children out of school and families and friends traveling to visit one another, the Christmas season is an ideal time to bring people together outdoors as well as indoors around the dining-room table or the Christmas tree.

Perhaps you are planning a tree-trimming party, an open house, or an informal dinner. Have you thought about organizing your party around an afternoon of outdoor activities that would be fun and invigorating for your guests?

Tobogganing

If you live in a region where the first snows of winter occur before Christmas, riding sleds and toboggans in your backyard or on a neighborhood hill is a fun activity for both children and adults.

Ice-skating

Ice-skating at a nearby pond or lake—or even at an indoor facility— is an enjoyable adventure.

Don't be put off by the fact that you are not in the same class as Scott Hamilton. For people who have never been on the ice before, pair them with a wooden chair that has a high back. It sounds—and looks— rather stupid, but even novices can get around remarkably well by holding onto the back and pushing the chair in front of them. Don't forget

Make good use of your time off work. Enjoy the snowy outdoors and plan activities for your family, such as building a snowman, opposite page.

*Transport yourself into
another century:
Taking a sleigh ride can be a
memorable
and romantic occasion.*

to bring along a transistor radio and plenty of thermoses of coffee and hot chocolate.

When everyone has collapsed with laughter, tired ankles, cold feet, and soggy mittens, invite them back to your house for hot cider, mulled wine, and Christmas confections.

Snow Sculptures

Many of us have childhood memories of bundling up in warm clothes and rushing outside into the nippy air to make angels in the snow and roll large snowballs to be stacked into snowmen. As part of a holiday gathering of friends and family, revive these feelings and give them a different twist.

Instead of making one simple snowman, have adults and children build several figures. Provide them with old hats and other items of clothing to dress their congregation of snow people and give them individual looks and personalities. Other sculptures can also be created in snow. Suggest to the crew of builders that they make a menagerie of snow animals—bears, cats, dogs, turtles, dinosaurs—to decorate your yard. Turn the activity into a game by seeing who can build the biggest or the most fanciful animal. Or, have a theme, and construct related shapes or figures. The sculptures can be decorated with food coloring diluted in water and then brushed onto the snow. Be sure that young children are paired with adults so they have help when necessary.

To commemorate the event, have a camera on hand, take pictures of your guests with their creations, and send them copies tucked in a Christmas card as a record of the day spent together. If you own an instant camera, you can present the photographs to your guests on the spot. Mugging for photographs can be a fun activity in itself.

House Trimming

Even if you can't count on pre-Christmas snowfall, you can still make outdoor activities a part of holiday celebrations. Invite guests to help decorate the exterior of your house or trim a tree in the front yard.

In warm or mild climates, hold your accompanying Christmas party outdoors. Take a lead from the Victorians, who developed the celebration of Christmas into a fine art. Favorite after-dinner pursuits included playing games such as pantomime and charades.

Caroling

No matter what part of the country you live in, caroling is a traditional activity enjoyed by people of all ages.

Although the oldest Christmas songs date from the early 1500s, it was the Victorians who gathered previously neglected carols and published them for the first time. Throughout England in the late 1800s, carolers roamed towns and cities during the holidays entertaining their friends and neighbors.

For your caroling group, the audience can be your neighbors, shoppers at the local mall, or patients in the hospital. In many communities, volunteers organize caroling evenings in order to collect money for charities and, at the same time, set the mood for the holidays by filling the air with the music of Christmas.

Tobogganing—on a garbage-can lid if you have nothing else—or making angel impressions in the snow are simple joys for both children and adults.

The Trees Of Winter

The heart, herald, and most familiar symbol of the holiday season

o term the Christmas tree a decoration, even the main decoration of the holidays, understates its importance as the center of Christmas in the home. It is the most imposing decoration and sometimes the only one. Festooned and bedecked with ornaments, it is situated in full view of family, visitors, and often passersby. This symbol of Christmas brings color, fragrance, life, light, and joy into the home.

Traditionally, the tree is the heart of Christmas. Gifts are spread and later exchanged under its boughs, and families and friends draw close around it to sing carols and join together in a celebration of the season.

In this chapter, after a look at the history and lore of the Christmas tree, you'll find a detailed discussion of popular species of trees, both cut and rooted, and instructions for their care. Useful information covers selecting a tree, keeping it fresh through the season, and safely disposing of it afterward. If you prefer a rooted, living tree, you will find how to select one and how to keep it healthy indoors.

Even for people living in the South and Southwest, snow-clad trees, preceding page and opposite page, is an image that comes to mind at Christmastime. And bringing home a tree you have cut yourself, left, is the wish of many.

Why a Tree?

From pre-Christian and probably prehistoric times to the present, the Christmas tree has played a significant part in many rituals and ceremonies. After centuries of use, a fascinating body of lore has developed around the tree.

Some of the earliest precursors of the Christmas tree were various evergreens used to affirm life, and in some cases light, in the darkest, bleakest time of the year.

During the winter solstice in prehistoric times, Celtic priests trimmed oaks with apples and burning candles to offer thanks to the gods who gave them sunlight and fruit. Ancient Romans celebrated the Saturnalia in mid-December and the Calends of January by dressing evergreen trees and branches with candles and decorations and sometimes by crowning the trees with representations of their sun god. In parts of northern Europe, observations of holidays at various times of the year included decorating evergreen trees. The first maypoles, for example, were ornamented evergreen trees.

Some legends date back to the arrival of Christianity in Europe. In the eighth century, St. Boniface came upon a group of Germans about to sacrifice a child beneath an oak sacred to Thor. Stopping the sacrifice, he felled the oak, revealing a small fir tree, which he proclaimed to be a symbol of Christ and the spirit of love that Christ embodies. Another legend holds that when Joseph of Arimathea brought Christianity to Great Britain, he tired as he climbed a steep hill on Christmas Eve. Stopping to rest, he pushed the end of his hawthorn walking stick into the ground. The stick burst into leaf and bloom, encouraging him to go forward with his mission. This tree, the Glastonbury thorn, is said to have been transplanted later to nearby Glastonbury Abbey, where various reputed offspring survive today.

According to a widely believed legend, Martin Luther created the first Christmas tree. Apparently, he was

This Mexican Tree of Life derives from the ones used in medieval plays performed at Christmastime.

walking outdoors on Christmas night when snow-covered trees sparkled in the moonlight and stars glinted through the branches overhead. Inspired by what he had seen, he returned home with a cut fir tree, a *Tannenbaum*, which he decorated with lighted candles for his family.

The Christmas tree as we know it descends directly from a representation of the Tree of Knowledge of Good and Evil in the Garden of Eden. It was featured in a traditional medieval mystery play performed on Christmas Eve within a circle of lighted candles. The enactment of the story of Adam and Eve culminated in their expulsion from Paradise. The play, however, ended optimistically with the promise of a savior sent by God who would be the incarnation of the Son of God. The evergreen tree, called the Paradise Tree, was hung with apples and symbolized the temptation and fall of Adam and Eve.

By the end of the fifteenth century, the church banned performances of mystery plays, but the only prop in the Paradise Play—the tree— began to appear in private homes in Germany. As the connotations of

It is difficult to improve on the ornaments hung by Mother Nature.

26

temptation disappeared, the Tannenbaum came to symbolize the promise of redemption offered by Christ. It was typically decorated not just with apples but with white Eucharist wafers representing salvation. (The same basic tree, called the *Paradeis*, survives to this day in some parts of Germany.) The Eucharist wafers later evolved into dough or pastry figures of angels, stars, hearts, and representations of people and various animals. Germans called this ornamented tree the *Christbaum*.

Another Christmas decoration used in German homes at the time of the Christbaum also figures in the evolution of the modern Christmas tree. When the Paradise Play was performed, candles surrounded the area in or near the church where the play took place. Because of their use in this and other religious contexts during Christmas, candles came to represent Christ, Light of the World.

When Christmas trees were first introduced into German homes, candles were placed on a *Lichtstock*, a pyramid of wooden shelves of graduated widths. Each shelf was flanked by burning candles, and the pyramid was topped with a candle. Typically, the Lichtstock was adorned with sprays of evergreens. Its triangular shape and fresh greenery suggested a tree. The shelves held a variety of Christmas decorations, sometimes including crèches. In a German household the Christbaum and Lichtstock were set up together on Christmas Eve. In many areas of Europe they are still placed side by side. In locations where the pyramid hasn't survived, the candles and decorations, or modifications of these ornaments, were transferred to the Christmas tree. These changes, which began in the mid-seventeenth century, eventually resulted in the lighted and lavishly ornamented Christmas tree of today.

Old and New World Christmas Trees

The first records of the *Christbaum* decorated with apples and wafers date from the beginning of the seventeenth century and come from Strasbourg, France. Cut fir trees, placed on tabletops, were decorated with pastry figures, ornaments made of sugar, and paper roses in many colors. During the latter part of the seventeenth century, candles were added, and many of the ornaments were gilded. Until the nineteenth century, in parts of Germany and Austria, Christmas trees were often suspended from the ceiling either upside down or right side up. By the

Before open spaces were protected, it was common practice to go out and cut down a tree.

late eighteenth century, members of royalty and the rich merchant class throughout most of Europe had opulent Christmas trees. In the early nineteenth century, the Christmas tree was widely adopted throughout Germany and much of Europe.

Evidence suggests that the English royal family used Christmas trees by the end of the nineteenth century. This disproves the popular legend that attributes the introduction of the Christmas tree in England to Prince Albert, the German-born husband of Queen Victoria. Prince Albert was, however, enthusiastic about Christmas trees. His angel-topped trees were lit with candles and adorned with many elegantly glazed and gilded sweets. These trees spread the practice of bringing a tree indoors during the Christmas season. In England, however, the scant supply of evergreens kept the Christmas tree from being commonplace. The fortunate enjoyed tabletop trees, which were also popular in other parts of Europe.

It is thought that the Christmas tree became established in some parts of the American colonies before it was widespread in much of Europe.

Moravians who had immigrated to Bethlehem, Pennsylvania, and Salem, North Carolina, in the early eighteenth century brought the custom of the Lichtstock (see page 27). The first Lichtstock in America appeared in 1717. According to legend, during the American Revolution, Hessian soldiers set up a Christmas tree in Trenton, New Jersey, inspiring many colonists to adopt the custom. However, this legend is not supported by documented fact.

By the early nineteenth century, Christmas trees were known in Boston, Philadelphia, and other American cities and towns, usually introduced by German immigrants. In 1832, Charles Follen, a German immigrant who taught at Harvard, set up a Christmas tree in his Boston home. Williamsburg, Virginia, is a town where colonial English-American Christmas decor has received wide attention. During the 1840s, advertisements in American newspapers urged people to pay admission fees to see decorated Christmas trees, and their popularity spread westward throughout the country. By the 1860s, decorated trees had reached the West and become common in San Francisco.

Incorporating a decorated tree in the American observance of Christmas was not always easy. For example, when German-born Reverend Henry Schwan set up a tree in his church in Cleveland, Ohio, in 1851, many members of the congregation protested vociferously that he was reviving a terrible pagan custom. Fortunately, another Cleveland minister interceded and appeased the congregation by sending a tree—a gift that could not be refused—to Reverend Schwan.

As evidenced on the opposite page, decorating trees has been customary for many years. Traditional garlands, left, are still popular.

Cut Trees

Every year, 32 million trees are cut on North American Christmas tree plantations for the United States market, and about 85 million young Christmas trees are planted for harvesting 6 to 12 years later. Only a small percentage of the trees marketed every year are natives; their removal serves to thin forest growth, giving more light, room, and nutrients to the remaining trees. Tree lots, choose-and-cut tree farms, and many plant nurseries that sell trees begin marketing them around Thanksgiving. Species offered for sale vary widely, even within some regions of the country.

Before you select and take home a tree, you should know the answers to some basic questions. What choices do you have? Which type of tree is best for your needs? What criteria should you use to select your tree? Should you cut your own at a tree farm or buy a ready-cut tree from a Christmas tree lot? How should you situate and care for your tree at home to assure freshness and to prevent fire? After the holidays, how should you dispose of the tree?

When cut Christmas trees were first marketed, in the second half of the nineteenth century, choices were relatively simple. People usually chose from among the few suitable kinds of trees that grew in their immediate area. With advances in modes of transportation and the cultivation of Christmas trees, a wider selection is now available.

Selecting a Tree

The appearance of each species is important to consider. Your selection should suit your tastes and needs. Consider the color and texture of

Trees that are brought to city lots have been carefully grown and harvested.

each type of tree and whether it conforms to your preferences. Bear in mind the kind of ornaments you will use. Do the ornaments require space beneath the branches in order to hang gracefully, or will they look best on the surface of a uniformly dense tree?

For most people who set up Christmas trees, durability figures high on the list of requirements for a suitable tree. This means buying a freshly cut tree. Before you buy a fresh specimen, you should know that some types of cut trees last far longer than others and, with proper care, are safer to keep in the house for longer than others.

Durability is not a major criterion if you keep a tree for only a few days. If, like most people, you expect to enjoy a tree for a week or more, you need to consider the length of time each candidate can be expected to last. The rule of thumb is that firs last the longest, pines are the next most durable, and spruces are by far the least durable.

Tree Plantations

Knowing something about Christmas tree production will help you to decide which option to choose, and to appreciate the growing, harvesting, and marketing efforts that have produced the tree you buy. This background knowledge will also answer questions you might have about the ecological implication of Christmas tree agriculture.

Most Christmas trees sold in the United States are grown on plantations, carefully tended, harvested, and prepared there for shipment. This relatively new type of agriculture is practiced in nearly every state and Canada. The Great Lake area, the Northeast, and the Northwest are leading producers of Christmas trees in the United States. Franklin D. Roosevelt was an early, and no doubt the most famous, owner of a Christmas tree farm.

Christmas tree farming differs from farming of most other crops in two basic ways: The period from planting to harvesting is 4, 6, or even 12 years rather than months. The other difference is that Christmas tree farming is often done on land unsuitable for other crops.

The long intervals between planting and harvesting mean that growers must wait years to recover their expenses and reap their profits. They also mean that farmers need to operate on a large enough scale that they can plant trees on different parts of their land every year to insure an uninterrupted supply of trees ready for harvest. Because tree

maturity rates vary, only some of the trees in any one field are harvested in one season.

For people who are concerned about the ecological aspects of cutting trees that will only be enjoyed for a few days before being discarded, the following benefits may be of interest: Christmas tree farms offer food and shelter to a wide range of wildlife; land too poor for other crops is often adequate, indeed ideal for some species; trees prevent erosion or retardation and add oxygen to the atmosphere.

Most growers buy seedlings from special nurseries and plant them 1,200 to 2,000 per acre. Christmas tree crops are subject to most of the same perils as most other agricultural crops, but for a period of many more years. As the trees grow, many tree farmers prune and shear to assure the best shape and density. Some species require little or no shearing, but others, such as Scotch pine and

Douglas fir, are commonly if not always sheared. In warm southerly climates, shearing is done up to 3 times a year; in northerly or higher-altitude areas where air is colder and the growing season shorter, shearing is done annually.

Usually in fall, trees earmarked for the current harvest are cut, sized and sometimes graded, then baled (bundled with their branches wrapped tightly against their trunks) and shipped to wholesalers or directly to retailers. New cold-storage technology allows early cutting and long storage of trees, a boon to growers in areas where early snows hamper or prevent later harvesting.

Many tree farms are open to the public.
Visiting a farm and choosing and cutting your own tree can be a memorable family outing.

33

Popular Pines

Pines make handsome Christmas trees whether they are cut trees purchased from a tree lot or live trees planted in the yard for year-round enjoyment and decorated as part of your outdoor Christmas display. For those who wish to plant pine trees, growing information is included in the descriptions that follow.

Pines, particularly sheared ones, are fairly dense with very little open space between branches for displaying hanging ornaments. Mature trees vary widely in shape and size.

Eastern White Pine
(*Pinus strobus*), native to the Northeast and the southern Appalachians, likes moist or dry, sandy soils that might be poor for other kinds of agriculture. Its slender, bluish green, 2-to-5-inch needles are soft and flexible. At maturity this pine is the largest conifer native to the Northeast, reaching 75 to 100 feet tall, with a pyramidal crown.

Western White Pine
(*Pinus monticola*) resembles its Eastern counterpart but has shorter, stouter needles. Where well adapted, it grows to 100 to 175 feet tall. When young, it makes an attractive Christmas tree.

Eldarica Pine
(*Pinus eldarica*), having adapted to desert regions of the Southwest from its native Caucasus Mountains of Russia, Afghanistan, and Pakistan, grows fast once established in open ground—up to 6 feet per year and to 50 to 65 feet in 10 years. It thrives on the heat, dryness, and alkaline soil of the desert and also accepts

Eastern white pine

coastal conditions. A variety called 'Christmas Blue Eldarica' is grown commercially in Arizona. Other common names for this species are Mondell, Afghan, and desert pine. The 5-to-6-inch needles are deep green.

Monterey Pine
(*Pinus radiata*), native to coastal areas of Central California, thrives in the cool summers and mild winters of its native fog belt. It accepts most soils but prefers well-drained, sandy loam and tolerates drought. Young trees

have shiny, bright green needles 4 to 6 inches long and grow in an attractively dense, pyramidal shape. Because growth is unusually rapid, trees may be harvested in 5 years. Mature trees range from 40 to 100 feet tall and have dense crowns.

Ponderosa Pine
(*Pinus ponderosa*) is native to wide areas of the West, particularly in mountainous regions. In youth and at maturity, it has a straight trunk and gracefully symmetrical branches. Where well adapted, it grows at a moderate to fast rate to 150 and even 200 feet tall, making it unsuitable for planting in most gardens. Bright yellow-green needles, which stand out stiffly, are 5 to 10 inches long. Ponderosa pine can be grown successfully in a container.

Virginia pine

Scotch pine

Scotch or Scots Pine
(*Pinus sylvestris*), native to parts of northern Europe and Asia and widely grown in North America, even in the coldest areas, prefers sandy soil and plenty of moisture. Short needles, 1½ to 2 inches long, are stiff and twisted. With shearing, Scotch pine is very bushy and dense, usually without open space between branches. Color varies in winter from bright to yellowish green. Mature trees are 75 to 100 feet tall. As a cut tree, the Scotch pine holds its needles longer than most pines.

Virginia Pine
(*Pinus virginiana*), native to the Southeast, adapts well to dry and poor soils that are unsuitable for many other plants. Similar in appearance to Scotch pine, it makes a shapely, fairly dense Christmas tree, with slender, stiff needles 1¼ to 3 inches long. Fast growth allows harvesting in 4 or 5 years. As a mature tree, it is 30 to 40 feet tall, irregular in shape with open growth and sparsely spaced branches.

They Needn't Be Pines

The following list covers the most popular species of Christmas tree other than pine. (For notes on pine trees, see the preceding two pages.) Because all of these trees are often used as living trees planted in containers, notes on their adaptability and cultivation are included.

Spruce

Native to cold climates, spruces are found in northerly and mountainous areas, even up to timber line, and stunted forms grow in the tundra. The four angled needles are short, stiff, and prickly, and they stick out from around the twigs. Sturdy branches provide ideal support for hanging ornaments. Mature trees tend to be tall and steeple shaped.

Colorado blue spruce

Colorado blue spruce: (*Picea pungens* 'Glauca'), native to forests in the Rocky Mountain area and usually found close to streams, is grown commercially in the same region. The silver-blue needles are 1 to 1½ inches long. Magnificent but not especially durable when cut, the blue spruce is nevertheless popular as a cut tree and is extremely popular to cultivate as a living tree. Planted outdoors, this spruce can grow to a height of 100 or 125 feet. A mature tree has a broad pyramidal shape with stiff horizontal branches.

Norway spruce

Norway spruce: (*Picea abies*), a northern and central European spruce, has adapted well on plantations in cool, humid climates of the Rocky Mountain area, the Northwest, the Northeast, and much of Canada. The needles, which point slightly forward, are light green. As a young tree, it makes a formal pyramid, but as it grows toward its maximum size of up to 150 feet, it becomes irregular in shape, with long, sweeping branches.

Cedar

The one species listed here is not a true cedar but a juniper. As is true of other junipers, it does not have cones but instead has bluish, berrylike fruits, which are eaten by birds.

Eastern red cedar: (*Juniperus virginiana*), native to the East and Midwest, prefers limestone areas but it thrives in forests with poor, rather dry soil and in fields. Growth is dense and shrubby. Branches are flexible and too weak to support many ornaments.

Young foliage is sharp and prickly with extremely short needles on four-sided twigs (handle the tree with heavy gloves). Needles on some mature trees lie flatter but are nevertheless sharp. Color is bright to dark green in spring and summer, purplish or reddish green at Christmas. Cultivated forms vary in color, ranging from dark green to bluish, silvery, or slightly gold tones. Trees grow rapidly to a variety of heights ranging from 10 to 30 feet tall and 5 to 10 feet wide. They are usually vase shaped or pyramidal.

Cypress

All American cypresses are native to areas of the West. Only one cypress is listed here. Its cones are spherical, woody, and about an inch in diameter.

Arizona cypress: (*Cupressus arizonica*), a native of Arizona and parts of northern Mexico, grows in poor, rocky, or sandy soil and tolerates harsh desert conditions but not extreme cold. This small, dense, uniformly conical tree has handsome bluish green foliage. It grows rapidly to a mature size varying widely from 20 to 60 feet. A mature tree may be open or dense; color changes to gray-green as tree matures.

Fir

All but one of the five trees described below belong to the genus *Abies*, natives of northerly and high mountain forests. Moist, cold, winter climates best suit them. Firs are symmetrical and usually pyramidal, with whorls of uniformly spaced branches. Their beauty and durability indoors, along with the strength and tiering of their branches, make them choice Christmas trees.

Balsam fir: (*Abies balsamea*), native to cool, moist habitats from Labrador to Minnesota and West Virginia, and grown commercially within this range, adapts poorly to gardens in other areas. The short, flat needles, rounded at the tips and measuring 1 to 1½ inches, are bright green with silvery undersides. They curl upward to crowd the upper sides of the twigs. Foliage forms soft, feathery sprays. At maturity, balsam fir reaches 40 to 75 feet and has a pyramidal shape. It is unusually aromatic.

Douglas fir or Montana fir: (*Pseudotsuga menziesii*), also very aromatic, isn't a true fir

Douglas fir

but has many of the virtues of fir. Native to moist, well-drained soils of British Columbia and the Northwest, the coast and Sierras of California, and the Rocky Mountain area, it is widely cultivated because of its pyramidal shape, fragrance, and rapid growth. When sheared, the trees are bushy and dense; unsheared, they are fairly open, with pliant branches. Needles are bright green or bluish green and 1 to 1½ inches long. At maturity, these firs reach 70 to 200 feet, and the branches droop and arch gracefully. As a tree ages, the lowest third of its trunk becomes bare.

Fraser fir: (*Abies fraseri*), native to small mountainous areas of North Carolina, Tennessee, and Virginia, is sometimes grown in similar climatic areas outside its natural range. Rich, moist, well-drained soil and a cool climate suit it. Short, dark-green, lustrous needles, ½ to 1¼ inches long, are twisted at their bases so they appear to be crowded on the upper sides of the twigs, much like the needles of

balsam fir, which this tree closely resembles. Fraser fir is a particularly good choice for a Christmas tree.

Noble fir: (*Abies procera*), native to cool mountain areas of California, Oregon, and Washington, where winters are wet and summers dry, has short, stiff branches spaced rather far apart, making it an excellent tree for hanging ornaments. Short (1-to-1½-inch) silvery needles turn upward and crowd the upper surfaces of the twigs. Mature height is 100 to 200 feet. Outside its natural habitat, this tree seldom grows satisfactorily.

Noble fir

White fir: (*Abies concolor*), from Rocky Mountain and Sierran habitats, has dense, bluish green, 2-to-3-inch-long needles that age to whitish green. Like most firs, it retains its perfectly tiered, pyramidal symmetry as it matures to 120 to 150 feet tall and its crown tapers into a sharp spire. Unlike other firs, it can tolerate dryness, heat, and smog.

Down On The Farm

In summer
sun,
in winter
snow

A dress of
green
you always
show

The first Christmas trees came wild from the forest, where every family went to cut its own tree. The age of the open forest has passed, and nowadays there are very strict regulations governing where you can and cannot fell trees. Today you must either buy a cut tree at a lot or cut your own at a choose-and-cut Christmas tree farm.

Across the country, in locations within reasonable driving distance of many cities, Christmas tree farms and sections of tree plantations are open to the public. Around Thanksgiving these farms start welcoming people to come and select and cut their own trees. If this source of buying Christmas trees is available to you, there are many advantages to taking a drive into the country to cut your own special tree.

Many families make the trip to the choose-and-cut farm an annual ritual to initiate the holiday season. The day includes a bracing country outing, the acquisition of a farm-fresh tree, and, perhaps best of all, the shared experience of choosing and cutting the tree that will become the central feature of the holiday celebration in their home.

The price of a choose-and-cut tree is lower than that of a ready-cut one, because many labor costs and overhead expenses have been eliminated. Most choose-and-cut farms provide saws and other necessary tools and materials for you to cut the tree, move it to your car, and attach it firmly and securely to the car roof.

Increasingly, choose-and-cut farms are adding features that make visiting them an especially enjoyable experience. Comfortable reception facilities at some farms enable everyone to enjoy food, warm beverages, and perhaps an open fire after the tree has been cut. Some farms even offer sleigh or cart rides, special Christmas displays, and other diversions such as Santa Claus and farm animals to amuse children. More and more choose-and-cut operations augment their income by selling foods (especially country specialties such as fruitcake, honey, and homemade jellies), Christmas decorations including ornaments, wreaths, and greens, and handicrafts and other gift items. Some farms encourage customers to make two annual trips, the first to buy a seasonal item such as a Halloween pumpkin and, while there, to choose and tag the tree that they will return to cut nearer to Christmas.

A major advantage of cutting your own tree is, of course, the guaranteed freshness of the tree. Not only does a fresh tree look better and make less litter in the house, but with proper care it lasts a long time and—most importantly—freshness minimizes the chance of fire.

Some farms invite the public to choose their trees before cutting time. Visitors are offered hay rides and Halloween pumpkins.

*Agreeing on the perfect tree is
a decision that
involves the entire family . . .*

*Sometimes it is the youngest
members who are
allowed the final say . . .*

*But generally it is up to dad
to pay for and
tie the tree to the car.*

Selecting a Tree

ppearance and freshness
are the two basic consid-
erations that should guide
you when selecting a tree.
This is true regardless of whether
you are purchasing your tree at a local tree lot or a choose-and-cut farm.

Appearance
When shopping for a tree, keep in
mind the type of ornaments that you
will hang on it. The fir, because of
the spaces between whorls of
branches, offers sturdy support for
ornaments of all kinds and plenty of
room to accommodate hanging ornaments. The pine, which is denser,
lends itself to decorations that sit
gracefully on or close to its surface.

Consider the general decor of your
home when picking a suitable tree.
The overall texture of a Scotch pine
tends toward boldness and informal-
ity, whereas a noble fir, with
symmetrical tiers, widely spaced
branches, and short needles, has a
finer textured, more formal look.
Various species differ in color as well
as in texture.

After you've weighed these
considerations, checked to see what

species are available, and settled on
the one that suits you best, how do
you select the specimen that looks
best for your purposes?

If the tree will be seen in the
round, you should select one that is
attractively full on all sides and
symmetrical from every angle. If you
are looking for a tree that will fill a
corner or a niche or stand close to a
wall, you may be able to find a less
expensive tree marked down because
of a sparse or irregular side that will
be hidden from view.

Be sure to note the desired height
for the tree, remembering to take the
stand into account and allowing for
removal of two inches or more from
the base of the tree. Determine an
appropriate width as well. Decide
whether you prefer low branches
that, weighted with ornaments, lie
close to the floor, or higher branches
that make room for gifts or decorations hung under the tree.

Realize that cut trees are baled for
shipment with the branches bent

upward and pressed close to the
trunk. When seen in the tree lot,
branches are still angled slightly upward but will bend downward with
time and the weight of ornaments.

Flocked Trees
Most retailers of cut trees offer trees
sprayed with latex paint, then covered with cellulose or rayon flocking
that simulates snow. As well as
white, you can buy trees decorated in
pastel colors and even two-toned
flocking. Metallic or mica glitter is
often an additional option.

If you want a flocked tree, inspect
all candidates carefully before buying
one. Sometimes flocking is used to
disguise poor natural color or damage that has caused discoloration or
loose needles. Although poor color is
unimportant, discoloration may indicate a lack of freshness. Noticeable
looseness of needles invariably means
that the tree is dangerously dry.

Holes are sometimes drilled into
trunks of sparse or lopsided trees,
branches are inserted, and the sur-
gery disguised with flocking. The inserted branches are unable to absorb
water and can't stay fresh very long.

A dried-out tree can be a safety hazard.
When buying a tree from a city lot, select one that looks fresh.

Play it Safe

The safest tree is a fresh, moist one; only a dried-out tree is a fire hazard. You must keep the tree fresh for as long as it remains indoors. It is also important to place combustible materials away from the tree and properly use safe tree lights.

Studies that were conducted by the Canadian government's forestry department and by the Connecticut Agricultural Experience Station in New Haven point up significant facts about the relationship between freshness and fire safety of trees.

One finding was that cut trees may be stored outdoors in cool, moist, shaded conditions for up to several weeks without damage—that is, without weakening their ability to draw water into their tissues. In fact, when bases are recut and placed in water, some kinds of properly stored trees recover their full moisture content. The base should be recut immediately and the tree placed in water, as described on page 41.

As part of this study, a fresh tree was touched by the flame of a bunsen burner but did not combust. After several seconds, the flame ignited only the foliage that it contacted directly, but the fire didn't spread. However, ignition time was almost instantaneous and combustion of the whole tree occurred when moisture of the tree was low.

Another finding showed that if a tree's water supply is interrupted for a day—for example, when a water-filled tree stand becomes empty—the tree dries out rapidly even after the water supply is replenished. A 6-to-8-foot tree in a warm room uses 3 to 4 quarts of water per day, at least for the first few days.

As far as the Connecticut scientists could determine, supposed flame-retardant additives were ineffective. Water containing any of these various additives appeared to be no better than tap water. In fact, some flame-retardant additives can actually contribute to potential fire hazard by blocking the water-conducting tissues of the trees and thereby hastening drying.

Although these studies didn't assess spray-on flame retardants, efficiency of these retardants has not been established conclusively. Only a commercial process whereby trees are completely immersed in retardant has proved to be somewhat effective.

Keeping a Tree Fresh

Follow the procedure below for selecting a tree and maintaining its freshness.

★ When possible, select a tree that you know has recently been cut. When stood upright and jarred against the ground, the tree should lose few, if any, needles. Note, however, that older needles on the inside of a healthy, growing tree die naturally but cling to it for a long time. So do older pine needles toward the bases of branchlets. Dropping of these old needles does not indicate that a tree isn't fresh.

Another test for freshness is to bend a needle gently between your fingers. If it is brittle and breaks, a tree probably isn't fresh; if it bends, a tree is fresh. Buying a fresh tree early and storing it with its recut base in water is better than, at the last minute, buying a dry tree that has likely lost its ability to draw water.

★ When you bring the tree home, cut off at least one inch from the base. A diagonal cut exposes a larger water-absorptive surface than a flat cut. Immediately stand tree upright with end completely submerged in fresh water. Use either a temporary container or a water-filled tree stand. Store tree in a place that is cool, shaded, windless, and humid, such as a basement or garage. Remember to keep container filled at all times. If you're likely to forget, post reminders to yourself. If it dries up temporarily before decoration, cut off another inch or more from the base before putting base back into water.

Thorough spraying of all foliage with an antidesiccant, available at nurseries, will retard transpiration (loss of water through foliage into air). This is usually unnecessary if a fresh tree is constantly kept in water, but it will help in hot and dry rooms.

★ Rather than moving the tree abruptly from a cold place into a heated living room, bring it into a cool location such as a basement or an enclosed porch the night before you decorate it. Before positioning it in the stand, cut at least another inch from the bottom, this time squaring off the earlier diagonal cut so tree will rest more securely in the stand.

★ Place tree as far as possible from heat ducts, radiators, fireplaces, television sets, and stoves.

★ Regularly monitor water level in stand and condition of tree. If tree becomes dangerously dry, consider taking it down immediately. However, careful selection and proper care should insure that a tree remains fresh for one to two weeks.

Some forethought when you set up a tree in the house can eliminate the problem of moving a shedding tree. An effective solution to a messy problem is to place a large plastic garbage bag beneath the tree stand. Fold it so that it functions as a skirt for the decorated tree. After emptying the stand with a turkey baster and removing the ornaments, the bag can be unfolded to contain the tree.

Disposing of a Tree

When the holiday season ends and it's time to take down the tree, you will be faced with the question of how to dispose of it.

A word of caution: Never attempt to cut up and burn a tree indoors in the fireplace. Dry foliage is extremely flammable and can instantly support a fire that might rage out of control.

The National Christmas Tree Association makes several suggestions for creative recycling of a Christmas tree, including using the needles in potpourri or aromatic fir pillows and sachets.

You can make mulch from the tree, using a wood chipper for the trunk. The branches can serve as a loose protective cover for perennials and small shrubs. As a mulch that will decay and build soil, conifer foliage is appropriate for garden plants that prefer acid soil.

Christmas trees make excellent sand barriers and retarders of erosion. At beach property or wherever there are gullies, a tree can be very beneficial.

In closing out the season, you can practice the old-fashioned custom of putting edible decorations on a tree, including candies, pastries, and nuts. If you establish a rule that these goodies can be eaten only when the tree comes down, the potentially dreary disassembly of the Christmas season can end on a sweet note.

If it is not done for you, remove the base and cut an inch off the trunk.

When purchased from a lot, trees usually have some kind of attached base.

A Deodar cedar (Cedrus deodara) planted in the yard can be enjoyed throughout the year as well as at Christmas.

ground or keep it healthy in its container for use Christmas after Christmas. Other practical matters, such as the need to move a heavy container, must also be considered.

When anticipating growth rates, bear in mind that a container culture stunts a tree. For example, an eldarica pine might grow up to 6 feet per year once established in the ground under ideal conditions. The same pine in a container would grow somewhere between one third and one half that rate. Also, the growth rate of a tree in a container slows and, in some cases, nearly stops as roots become crowded.

Of the major groups, pines grow fastest in containers or the ground, spruces far less rapidly, and most firs are a bit slower than spruces. One exception is the Douglas fir, which grows faster than firs and spruces, but slower than most pines.

Aleppo pine: *(Pinus halepensis)*, native to the Mediterranean region, is hardy only in southerly areas and adapts to Southern California and desert areas of the Southwest. Its form is open and graceful, and the gray-green needles sparse and feathery. Planted in the ground, it grows rapidly to 30 to 60 feet and spreads 20 to 30 feet; growth rate is slower, however, than that of eldarica and Monterey pines.

Deodar cedar: *(Cedrus deodara)*, native to low elevations of the Himalayas, grows fast to 80 to 150 feet and spreads to 40 to 60 feet under ideal conditions. A tree in a container usually grows under 1 foot a year. The soft texture is created by clusters of 1-to-2-inch needles that range from bright green to yellow-green. The pyramidal form, with gracefully drooping branches, makes this one of the most unusual and handsome trees for container or garden. If you plant it in the ground, allow plenty of room for growth. The deep root system fares best in a deep container.

Living Trees

Living Christmas trees growing in containers are becoming an increasingly popular alternative to cut trees. In using them, many advocates feel they are saving, rather than sacrificing, trees for Christmas.

Popular Species

If you prefer a living to a cut tree, you need to examine what species are available and, of those, which are best suited to the local climate, which appeal most to your tastes, how to select a specimen, and how to care for it indoors. You must decide whether to plant and maintain the tree in the

Dwarf Alberta spruce: also called dwarf white spruce (*Picea glauca* 'Conica'), a beautiful pygmy, is ideal for a container because of its slow growth rate (3 to 4 inches a year at first, slowing as tree ages), its dense, fine, short foliage, and its solid, pyramidal form. Even when planted in the ground, this native of Canada reaches only 7 to 10 feet in 40 years. It thrives in cold areas and adapts to most conditions except the hot desert climates.

Italian stone pine or umbrella pine: (*Pinus pinea*), native to the Mediterranean area, is bushy and rounded in youth; as an older tree up to 40 to 70 feet tall, it has a flat, spreading crown atop a sturdy trunk. The glossy, bright green needles, 4 to 7 inches long, are very dense on the branches. In a container the tree grows about 1 foot a year; in the ground it grows at a moderate rate for a pine. Like aleppo pine, it is unsuitable for very cold climates but tolerates dry heat and drought. (All trees in containers need fairly regular watering because the soil dries out in a container and the roots are unable to extend down to a moist zone.)

Japanese black pine: (*Pinus thunbergiana*), from Japan, is quite hardy and tolerates a wide range of conditions, including sea spray and desert heat. In the ground it grows fast to 90 or 100 feet high and assumes varied, irregular shapes. More than nearly any other tree, however, it is malleable: Grown in a container or the ground, it can easily be encouraged into almost any shape by pruning, and its usual growth of 1 to 2 feet per year in a container can be slowed considerably by pruning. The stiff, bright green needles are 3 to 4½ inches long.

Other Possibilities
In addition to these five trees and the trees listed and described on pages 34–37, see what possibilities are offered at local nurseries. You may find other pines, spruces, and firs, as well as upright junipers (for example,

some varieties of *Juniperus chinensis*, *J. scopulorum*, and *J. virginiana*), dwarf forms of plume cedar (*Cryptomeria japonica*), Atlas cedar (*Cedrus atlantica*), and umbrella pine (*Sciadopitys verticillata*, not to be confused with *Pinus pinea*).

Selecting a Living Christmas Tree
Living Christmas trees, as sold at nurseries and other outlets, fall into two groups: field-grown trees and container-grown trees. In some cases you can't tell the type of a tree by sight, so shop at a reputable outlet and ask questions.

A tree that has been in a container for a long time may have crowded roots coiled into a tight, rigid mass, which means loss of the vigor, fullness, and lushness found in an unwilted, prime field-grown specimen. If roots are not matted or do not protrude at the surface of the soil, and if the tree is full and has a

healthy color, you can be fairly sure that is in good shape.

Container-grown trees
The difference between this tree and a field-grown tree is time—a period of one to several years during which the tree has adapted to the container and its roots have reached through into the new soil. If you check the soil around the base of a tree, you can determine whether the burlap is new (and the tree was therefore field grown) or rotting (implying that the tree was container grown).

The container-grown tree that has spent its whole life in a container more clearly deserves the label. It originated as a seedling or a rooted cutting in a container and does not have roots wrapped in burlap.

A spruce in a container can be brought inside and decorated at Christmastime.

Containers check the growth of a tree and keep it to a manageable size.

Field-grown trees

These trees are grown in the ground, as the name indicates, then dug up and shipped. The roots of a field-grown tree are bound in burlap. The tree will be sold either in this form or with the burlap-covered roots set into a container and covered with soil. Examining a container-grown tree around the soil line will most likely reveal whether the roots are in burlap—but it will not tell you about the condition of the roots.

The least desirable possibility is that a field-grown tree has been dug within the past several months, even weeks, and that much of its root system has been cut away in the process. A tree handled in this manner needs at least a year to adapt fully to its container; if root loss has been severe, it is too soon to know whether a recently unearthed tree will survive in good form or at all. The stress caused by relocation of the tree to the warm, dry indoor temperatures during Christmas, then back out into the cold outdoors, will almost certainly

kill it unless the root system is intact and other conditions are favorable.

A far more promising possibility is that the grower prepared the tree at least a year in advance of replanting it. By using a spade or tool with a sharp blade to cut deep into the soil in a circle around the tree—perhaps twice, at intervals many months apart—a grower can force the tree to develop a dense, compact root system. Risk of serious damage or death to the tree is slight if this operation is performed at the proper time of year and soil is moist. Because the tree is left in place, uncut roots, including some delicate feeder roots, aren't broken or exposed to drying air. A year later, when the tree is unearthed and the roots are wrapped in burlap, the tree sustains only minor loss of roots if it is handled properly. It then has an excellent chance of survival.

Handle with Care

With proper handling and care, a wisely selected living tree should serve you well for many years. But it is important to know how to care for it indoors and outdoors, how to move it easily without harming it, and how to protect your floors. These and other bits of information assure that you will enjoy a living tree during Christmas and year around.

Selecting a Container

A living tree may come in a sturdy, durable, attractive container. If you buy it in burlap and unplanted, or if the nursery container is temporary or unappealing, you'll need to buy a container.

Wood, terra-cotta, ceramic, and plastic planters are widely available. Because a terra-cotta container is porous and loses water by wicking and evaporation from the outer surface, it requires more frequent watering than do other containers. Some woods—redwood, cypress, and teak, for example—are long lasting; others, such as pine and fir, will decay faster. Thick wood planters provide the best insulation.

If you buy a tree in burlap without a container, select a container large enough to accommodate the ball of roots with room to spare, but not so much room that the planter is disproportionately large and ungainly or unnecessarily heavy.

Whatever the type or size of the new container, it must have one large or several small drainage holes. Otherwise, roots will quickly rot. If

Garden-supply shops offer a variety of containers in which you can plant trees.

you find a ceramic container such as a Chinese egg jar without drainage holes, make them with the appropriate drill bit. Many garden centers that sell containers will drill drainage holes for a small fee.

Remember that the tree will have to be rolled or carried. Sturdy handles are an asset, unless a container is too heavy to lift. Some large wooden planters have built-in casters. Nurseries and garden centers also sell dollies that can remain permanently beneath planters; only a dolly with drainage holes is appropriate for your purposes. You may need a hand truck in order to move a heavy planter up steps or over uneven surfaces.

A note of caution: Whenever you lift a living tree, never grasp it by the trunk. The weight of the roots, combined with that of the planter, can and usually will break the roots. Move living trees by lifting the wrapped root ball or the planter.

Indoor Care

Indoor trees in planters have the same basic requirements as cut trees. To survive in good form, they need even more careful treatment than cut trees, which will be discarded afterward.

Ease the tree indoors by first placing it for a couple of days on a cool porch or in a bright garage. Later use the same method to reacclimatize the tree to the out-of-doors. In the house, situate the tree away from heat sources and drafts, preferably in a spot where it receives bright light from a window.

A living tree demands constantly moist, but well-drained, soil to survive its term indoors and to remain safely noncombustible. Water thoroughly one day before bringing the tree indoors. In the house, place the planter in a saucer, pan, or other receptacle large enough to catch drainage water, because you will need

to monitor the moistness of the soil and add water as needed—probably every couple of days. Most nurseries and garden centers sell large, deep plastic saucers. Never allow planter to stand in water that has drained from it; a turkey baster is useful for removing water.

As you situate the tree and then decorate it, be sure to leave access to the top of the planter, for watering, and to the drainage saucer, for removing water. To protect floor and furniture from water stains, avoid using an unglazed terra-cotta saucer (water seeps through eventually).

If a tree or plant is regularly outdoors, never bring it directly into a heated home. Ease it in by first putting it into a bright but cool room.

CHAPTER 3

Baubles Bangles & Beads

Dress the star of the show from top to toe

Even if the tree you purchased is a last-minute Cinderella—an orphan left in the lot because it was slightly misshapen—by the time it is dressed in its Christmas finery it will be ready for the ball. Decked out in ornaments, clad in tinsel, and crowned with a star, your tree will sing out the joy of Christmas to all who draw near.

No doubt you have boxes of ornaments—tokens and mementos of Christmases past—stored in the attic, basement, or garage. But maybe this year is the time to take stock, be more selective, and create a theme tree, a second tree, or a tree created specially for the children.

In this chapter you will find ideas for all kinds of trees—from formal to fun. There are theme trees, trees wrapped in ribbons and bows, and color coordinated. Read about the history of ornaments for added inspiration and see the ideas for decorations that you and the children can make. And don't forget the area around the base of your tree; it needs decorating too.

Before you are too caught up in the spirit and dash off to start hanging ornaments, see Lighting the Christmas Tree on page 136. The lights should go on first.

A tree covered in Christmas finery will always steal the show, whether it is put in a formal reception room, preceding pages, or in a cozy living room, right. Involve the children, left, when decorating.

The Dear Old Tree

BY LUELLA WILSON SMITH

There's a dear old tree, an evergreen tree,
And it blossoms once a year.
'Tis loaded with fruit from top to root,
And it brings to all good cheer.

For its blossoms bright are small candles white
And it's fruit is dolls and toys.
And they all are free for both you and me
If we're good little girls & boys.

From St. Nicholas magazine, December 1907.

Color Control

When making a theme tree, start out with only one or two ideas or colors so that you don't obscure the theme with too many colors, materials, and objects. A very simple, elegant tree can be made by restricting the type, color, and shape of the decorations.

The special features of a tree are dramatized by decorating it with only two or three colors of lights or bows and ribbons, or shaped ornaments such as globes, hearts, or stars. When choosing colors, consider which ones will look attractive together and be compatible with the interior of your home. Also, if the tree will be seen from outdoors, use ornaments in colors and sizes that will be visible from a distance.

The Natural Look

If you live in or access a rural area, you can collect flowers, herbs, or unusual vegetation and dry and preserve them yourself for the holidays. If you live near the ocean, save shells, driftwood, and other beachcombing treasures, and use them to give your Christmas tree a local flavor.

Yum-Yum Trees

Food makes a festive—and potentially delectable—motif for a Christmas tree. Traditional items such as cranberries and popcorn strung into garlands, candy canes, and cookie cutouts in a variety of shapes are still appealing decorations that can be made at home.

Other edibles can be combined with or replace these traditional items. One possibility is a cookie tree festooned with actual cookies and the cutters used to make them. Many cookie cutters are manufactured with handles through which a bow can be tied to form a loop for hanging. Making the cookies as well as decorating the tree can be a family project.

Fruits and vegetables are a good-looking, colorful combination. Fresh produce can be quite heavy, difficult to mount on a tree, and, of course, is perishable. Therefore, use wax or plastic reproductions, or find or make ornaments in the shapes and colors of specific fruits and vegetables. To this cornucopia tree, you can carry out the food theme by adding items such as nuts in their shells, small wooden kitchen spoons, and miniature molds.

And for a sweet-looking—and tasting—tree, try arranging candies in miniature baskets. Cover the tree with these treats and make sure you have plenty of extra candies to replenish empty baskets.

Make children feel special by decorating smaller trees and setting them up in their rooms. A favorite teddy bear can enjoy a front-row seat.

Toys and candy canes make
lively decorations that
children identify
with. Decorations can be dug
out of the toy box or
made specially for the tree.

55

Even though a decorated tree dominates and overshadows the general decor and flavor of a room, it should be in keeping with the mood and the theme. In a formal or traditional setting, a formal and traditional tree has the most appropriate appearance. Placement is also important. A tree should be positioned where it can be in full view most of the time yet not where it will get in the way. Consider the regular traffic patterns in your home and avoid placing the tree where it will interfere. The tree in the corner of an entrance hall, opposite page, is in full view yet out of the way. Sectional seating protects the tree, above. Mirror-backed shelves reflect the tree in a corner of the room, below.

The same element
repeated throughout a tree
(even if the
individual ornaments are
not identical) can be
very effective.
The tree in a formal living
room, right, is decked
out with sprays
of dried flowers that can
be used to fill in
any bare spots. It rises
from a base
swathed and tied similarly
to the drapes. Large
bows are the
theme used on the tree,
opposite page.
These can be tied from
pieces of wide
satin ribbon, colored crepe
paper, or fabric torn
into strips on the bias.

Miniature teddy bears cover a tree that is framed in the archway, above. Flexible joints on these bears mean that they can be arranged so they actually sit on the branches of the tree.

You can set a mood by the way in which you decorate a tree. The tone can be formal, or it can be charming, amusing, or whimsical. It can also be romantic, as evidenced by the trees on these two pages. Placed in a bedroom decorated with Victorian furnishings, opposite page, the flocked tree is as soft and pretty as the pile of cushions on the bed. What's more, the occupants will also be able to enjoy Christmas morning unwrapping parcels in bed. Romance is also the theme of the tree at left. Tiny baskets are filled with floral offerings. Make sure your Christmas purchases include several yards of ribbon. Not only can this be used for gift-wrapping, it can be tied into bow ornaments or, as seen here, hung streamer-fashion from the top of the tree.

Invented Trees

Unlike an artificial tree that strives to look like the real thing, an invented tree is a flight of fantasy. Often, the conical outline is the only thing that suggests a traditional evergreen. Sometimes even this tapering shape is ignored.

Invented trees can be made out of cones of Styrofoam or the floral foam used for dried flowers, available from florists or floral-supply companies. They can be covered with delicate sprigs of evergreen, then festooned with lilies, berries, pinecones, ribbons, and finely textured flowers—both fresh and dried. (Florist's water tubes will keep fresh flowers from wilting and can be hidden among other decorations.) Think of the foam cones as unpainted canvases to be filled in with whatever suits your taste and purpose. Whether you use dried flowers, tiny toys, seashells, or herbs together with cookies in various shapes, you will find many ways to evoke Christmas with diverse techniques and materials.

Another idea, appropriate for a serving table, celebrates Christmas and its bounty with a pyramidal array of fruits, vegetables, berries, foliage, and dried pods. Both cones are topped with pineapples, which are a

As long as the overall shape is recognizable, horns, top, pots of poinsettias, above, and a dried flower arrangement, right, can suggest Christmas trees.

When dreaming up a Christmas alternative to an evergreen tree, ingenuity is the name of the game. This one may look more like a maypole but, in December, everyone will know what it symbolizes.

traditional emblem of hospitality often displayed in the holiday decor of Colonial Williamsburg and other east-coast settlements.

You need not limit your creativity to the confines of a conical design. A wonderfully gnarled, dead manzanita branch, painted white or left natural, can be hung with Christmas ornaments to make an unusually shaped tree. A dried stalk of yucca or agave,

or any other appealing branch or stalk, offers the same possibilities.

Don't overlook the charm of topiaries, living or artificial. A container-grown topiary can be brought indoors and treated as a living Christmas tree.

Artificial Trees

Although a Christmas tree usually conjures up the image of an evergreen conifer decorated with electric lights, glass balls, and maybe tinsel, there are other kinds of trees. They are as wonderfully varied as the creative individuals who make them.

Practicality often plays as large a role as beauty in the choice of a tree. Nothing is more practical than a tree that demands little care, avoids causing worry, makes no mess, and can be used year after year.

Like the best artificial flowers, artificial Christmas trees have come a long way. The cleverest look like real evergreens even at close range; unlike real evergreens, they can be packed away and reused.

There are situations when a wire skeleton covered with green, flame-retardant synthetic foliage might be more appropriate than a cut or live tree. A room in a hospital or convalescent home is one such situation. Artificial Christmas trees range in size from small tabletop trees to floor models up to ten feet tall. Some are plastic and have detachable branches. Some come apart for easy storage and can be assembled by fitting large panels together by matching color-coded fittings. Others have hinged branches. Many use a bottlebrush-type construction with branches that can be bent and shaped. Some are molded. Much artificial foliage is now polyester, which makes it soft and pliable.

Flocked artificial trees can be particularly convincing replicas of snow-covered evergreens. On the best artificial trees, flocking is firmly bonded and permanent.

The Trimmings

Glass ornaments, made in Germany and Czechoslovakia, were highly prized on American trees in the late 1800s.

Victorian cards and decals, either cut out or framed in lace, are as popular on modern trees as they were in the late 1800s.

Each holiday season the real excitement begins when the ornaments from Christmases past are brought out from storage. The thrill of unwrapping and rediscovering familiar treasures is great, and it can inspire a wish to acquire new ornaments or to create decorations to add to the family collection.

Some of the first tree trimmings we learned to make as children—and may still make as adults—originated from the earliest celebrations of Christmas in this country by immigrants who introduced the traditions of their native lands.

Before ornaments were commercially manufactured and distributed, trees were embellished with readily available decorations that could not be kept for the following year. These ornaments included food, fruit, and other perishables.

In the German communities of Pennsylvania, trees were decorated with thin cakes or *Springerle* cookies molded in the shape of animals and flowers. Many families—each making an effort to fashion a unique shape—created their own cookie cutters.

Stringing garlands of popcorn and cranberries dates from the early 1800s. Making these decorations was a pastime that brought together family and friends. As the practice continued, variations were introduced: Popcorn was dyed with food coloring, and balls of caramelized popcorn were created for hanging from tree branches. Small homemade cornucopias filled with candies or nuts transformed early Christmas trees into feasts for both the eyes and the palate.

Christmas decorations were introduced to the United States at the end of the nineteenth century from Germany, the country where the first decorated Christmas trees appeared. Cast tin, wax, and cardboard shapes embossed with intricate details were among the first decorations to be imported and sold in America. Even though these were very popular, it was the glass ornaments from Germany and Czechoslovakia that became the most sought-after decorations in the late 1800s.

Although everyone has undoubtedly heard of the Woolworth five-and-dime stores, few people know that F. W. Woolworth, founder of the chain stores, was instrumental in popularizing German glass ornaments in the United States. At first skeptical—believing that they would be hard to sell and that they would break before they left the shelves—he ordered a modest $25 worth of stock for his Lancaster, Pennsylvania, store prior to the

Christmas of 1880. In two days the store was sold out. Woolworth made a trip to Germany, where he bought more than two hundred thousand ornaments. The town he visited, Lauschau, began making ornaments in the 1840s and provided practically all blown-glass decorations until the time of World War I.

The kinds of decorations that were used to embellish trees one hundred years ago provide ideas for the ornaments you can make for this year's tree. In addition to stringing popcorn and cranberries, create chains with links of colored and patterned paper—metallics are particularly festive because they reflect light. You can copy the German and Victorian custom of hanging various-shaped ornaments filled with candy. Construct

small paper or fabric cones or cornucopias or use small baskets and fill them with nuts and candies.

Some of the earliest German ornaments were made of cardboard cut out in the forms of birds, boats, fish, and Christmas figures. You, too, can make cutouts, collage them with lace, fabric, and decals, and draw on details with paint or colored markers. Ideas for these figures can be used to make your own cookie cutouts—surely the most delicious decorations to be found on a Christmas tree.

Fine porcelain heads are still to be found in antique stores and can be decorated to resemble this antique ornament.

Strings of beads, above,
are looped from
branch to branch to fill in
any bare spots before
the ornaments are hung.
Although the pinecones,
poinsettias, apples,
flowers, and bells, above
right, have little in
common,
they are each used often
enough to give the
tree a well-planned look.
The overall effect is
a red and
white color scheme.
Reminiscent of icicles, the
glass and clear
plastic ornaments frost
every branch of
the tree,
right. Glass ornaments,
like the ones on
the opposite page, are ideal
for a tree designed to
sparkle with light.

Heirloom Globes

Studded with colorful beads and sequins and festooned with attractive ribbons, these Christmas ornaments can be given to friends and relatives, who will surely treasure them year after year.

Be sure to wear goggles when working with Styrofoam: Particles get into the air and can cause eye infections.

Making a Globe
The foundation for the decorations shown is a Styrofoam ball which can be found in garden centers, art-supply stores, and hobby shops. Decorative materials are attached to the ball with straight pins; use those with either plain metal heads or colorful plastic heads. Both types easily penetrate surface materials as well as the ball.

Completely cover the ball with sequins and beads of different colors and shapes, threading them onto straight pins. Make sure the head is large enough so that it does not pull through. Also check that the pinpoints do not stick out the other end; if they do, nip off ends with pliers.

Embroidered or velvet ribbons are easier to tie than are the synthetic ones sold for gift-wrapping.

The sphere is only one of many forms available. By exploring the stores in your

area, you can find Styrofoam in other shapes. You can also buy the material in sheets and cut whatever shapes you desire: triangles, stars, or animals. Because Styrofoam crumbles easily, the cleanest way to cut it is with an electric carving knife. A utility knife, serrated kitchen knife, or piece of wire will also do. To cut complex shapes, first make a paper pattern and pin it to the Styrofoam to use as a guide.

To make a hanger for a sphere, wrap and pin a length of ribbon vertically around it, and tie a bow at the top. Leave the ribbon long enough so that you can tie another bow for hanging the ornament, or attach a loop or a hook for hanging. As an alternative to ribbon, push a colorful pipe cleaner right through the center of the ornament. Twist the top end into a loop and thread the bottom end around a bead to prevent ornament from slipping off the pipe cleaner. Large balls completely covered with beads, sequins, and ribbons can be heavy; make small sizes for tree decorations.

Interest the whole family in creating these mosaics of color and texture, providing, of course, that children are old enough to handle sharp pins and small objects. Each year before Christmas, set aside time to add to your collection. Who knows: They may become family heirlooms.

Eggs, either blown or cooked, can be painted and hung together with chile peppers and corn on a tree decorated with a southwestern theme.

Handmade Ornaments

Many of the ornaments that are hung on a tree have folklore significance such as the Ukranian custom of having a spider and web. According to legend, a poor woman with nothing to put on her tree awoke on Christmas day and watched the morning sun turn cobwebs into delicate, silver tracery. More often, it is the local flora that dictates the way people decorate.

Chile Peppers

In the Southwest it is quite common to find chile peppers used for more than seasoning the local food. Often, they are braided like strings of garlic and treated as a decoration until the cook has used up the supply. As these bright red peppers can be found in specialty stores at this time of year, you can use them to spice up your Christmas tree, tie onto wreaths, weave into garlands, or just mound in a glass bowl. To emphasize the southwestern theme, add Indian corn, dried corn, and maybe a corn-husk doll.

To continue a Native American theme, you can have fun by painting hard-cooked eggs in appropriate colors and patterns. (If you plan to keep your egg ornaments, blow out the raw innards through a pinhole rather than cooking the egg.)

Clay-Dough Ornaments

This clay-like dough is ideal for making ornaments. Use any tools that seem appropriate to shape the dough. These might include cookie cutters and toothpicks.

Shaped dough ornaments can be painted after they are baked or food coloring can be added to the water with which you make the dough. If tinting the water, it is better to make small amounts of dough in several different colors rather than using the full recipe.

4 cups flour
1 cup salt
1 cup water
Food coloring (optional)
Aluminum foil
Ornament hangers or metal
*   paper clips*

1. Blend flour and salt in a large bowl. Add food coloring to the water (if desired). Add the colored or plain water gradually to form a firm dough. Knead dough until it is smooth.
2. Shape dough into ornaments and lay on foil-covered baking sheets. Carefully push in hangers. Or, cut paper clips in half widthwise and push in one half to act as a hanger.
3. Cook for about 2 hours at 250° F. Ornaments should be firm. Correct baking time will depend on the size and thickness of the dough.

Origami

Although they did not celebrate Christmas, this ancient art of paperfolding had a ceremonial function in folk religion in medieval Japan. The way to make flowers, birds, and animals by folding a piece of paper has been passed down through generations and the traditional shapes are made in exactly the same way today as they were hundreds of years ago.

Special patterned papers are available in craft and hobby stores but it is the folding of the paper that is important, not the paper itself. If you can't find origami paper, use wallcovering, gift wrap, colored foil, or even newspaper.

Hang your origami ornaments on the tree individually, string them into chains, or attach them to gift packages. Or, delight your dinner guests by turning a stiffly starched napkin into an origami rose.

Folded paper ornaments, above, are made using the Japanese art of origami. The angel, left, was modeled in clay dough and coiffed with hair made from dough squeezed through a garlic press.

Sheet Music Ornaments

Just looking at a tree with a music theme brings to mind the sounds of Christmas—favorite carols and melodies from The Nutcracker Suite.

These easy-to-make ornaments merely require sheet music plus readily available materials. They will fill your tree with the harmony of music as you and your friends sing the sounds of Christmas.

Following this procedure you can make variations by selecting alternatives to the materials shown here. Edge trim and ribbon ties can be in any color or any material, such as wrapping paper or fabric. All kinds of fresh or artificial foliage can also be used to decorate the scrolled sheet music. Or, attach differently shaped ornaments (consider miniature instruments).

To have even more fun with this project, and to create a game to play on Christmas Eve, decorate scrolls with materials and objects that provide a clue to the piece of music that is rolled up. Whoever correctly identifies the most titles, gets a prize that has been wrapped and placed beneath the tree.

You can get much inspiration by viewing store displays. The idea for making the sheet music ornaments, opposite, came from seeing this tree in the window of a San Francisco gift store.

1. Sheet music can be purchased or taken from songbooks you have on hand. You also need black construction paper (or opaque, colored adhesive tape), a straightedge, a craft knife, glue, assorted ribbon, foliage, and hat pins.

3. Glue lengths of black paper trim to the top and bottom edges of the sheet. Allow glue to dry thoroughly.

If you prefer, use colored or patterned adhesive tape. This eliminates the need to cut and paste strips of paper.

6. Using ribbon in a contrasting color, attach foliage, a bell-shaped ornament, or other decorations of your choice. Secure wherever necessary with a hat pin pushed through the sheet or with a straight pin with a colored head.

2. The sheet music looks attractive when given a finished edge. From the black construction paper, cut strips to the desired size (approximately ¼ to ¾ inch in width, and long enough to reach at least two thirds of the way across the top and bottom of the sheet). To ensure clean edges, cut paper with a straightedge and craft knife, rather than with scissors.

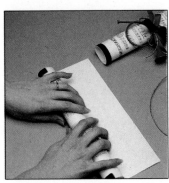

4. Roll sheet into a scroll, beginning at an edge not covered by the black border.

7. Trim the ends of the ribbon into a notched or other decorative pattern.

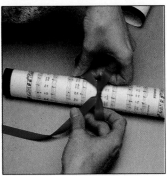

5. Using a square knot, firmly tie a length of ribbon into a bow to keep the cylinder rolled up.

8. To suspend the ornaments rather than resting them on the branches, add a hook.

*A halo of lights, obscured
behind a straw
starburst, adds to the charm
of the angel, above.
The ornaments, right, can be
wired to a tree that has
a straight and slender tip.*

Tree Toppers

W hether in a Christmas tree
lot, a tree farm, or a forest
setting—and regardless of
whether it is 6 foot or 60
foot—a fir or pine has a natural
pyramidal shape that leads the eye
toward its crown. When a tree is
decorated for Christmas, the lights
wound around its girth and the garlands draped from its branches create
a spiral that draws attention to the
peak of the tree—a special place that
deserves a special decoration.

Like many of the customs and objects used at Christmas, the top of
the tree has symbolic meaning. Because the star of Bethlehem is the
most obvious reference, many

commercially produced decorations
for the treetop evoke the star that lit
the heavens on that historic Christmas Eve centuries ago. These delicate
tree toppers are often made of the
thinnest glass. Sometimes etched
with designs and often painted with
jewellike colors including gold and
silver, they are transformed into
heavenly bodies as they reflect the
surrounding lights of your home.

The spire pictured here, like other
starlike designs available at Christmas, has a hollow extension intended
to be inserted over the slender tip of
the tree. These toppers often require
a tree with a top that is straight and
thin—which does not always occur
in nature or even in trees cultivated
at tree farms. However, a straight
stick or other armature can easily be

attached to the top of a tree to
accommodate the shaft of the ornament. Wrapping the armature in
tissue or cotton batting provides a
snug fit while protecting the fragile
glass from breakage.

Consider the size of the tree and
its location in your home. If a tree
reaches almost to the ceiling, decorations have to be large or colorful
enough, and properly lit, to be seen
clearly from eye level. For a tree
placed in the middle of a room,
rather than in a corner or against a
wall, use a tree topper that can be
enjoyed from all sides, sparking your
imagination to create a small-scale

merry-go-round of beautiful objects and special effects.

Choosing a crowning ornament for your Christmas tree should be approached with as much fun and imagination as when creating a theme tree or when deciding what to put at the base of a tree (see page 76). Toppers can dramatically punctuate a motif begun in the lower portions of the tree. On a tree hung with angels, the obvious topper is also an angel. On a tree festooned with ribbon, a large, red and green bow would be an appropriate crown.

The decoration on the top of a Christmas tree need not be confined to a single ornament. Whatever the theme of your tree—animals, bows, Santa Claus, food, toys—and whether the mood is elegant or playful, a grouping of thematically related or contrasting items makes a striking and creative way to finish off a tree. The apex can also be the point from which other decorations radiate. Elegant ribbon streamers or strands of beads and baubles can begin at the top of a tree and be draped all the way to the base. Rather than mounting miniature lights around the circumference of a tree, attach them so they hang in vertical rows that provide a counterpoint to the horizontality of the branches and form a lighted path pointing the way to the top.

If you don't have an ornament worthy of the attention it will get at the top of the tree, make one by twining strands of beads with a string of lights. Wrap the uppermost foot or two of the trunk so that only the ends of the short branches are visible as they protrude from the mass of glitter and light. Or, invite your daughter to dress her prettiest doll in its best dress and place it in the seat of honor at the top of the tree.

If you want to make your own ornament, materials of almost any type can be attached to a Styrofoam or cardboard base, formed or cut to the shape you desire. A wood or wire armature like that recommended on the opposite page should be incorporated to secure the ornament to the tree.

Think of a tree topper as an unfolding flower. The stem or vertical support can be covered with fabric or ribbon to make it decorative as well as functional. As for the flower, it can be as elaborate as a mixed bouquet of dried roses or glass balls, as fanciful as a huge bow tied with ribbons in all colors, or as simple as a lone bird about to take flight.

Angels
we have heard
on high,

Sweetly
singing o'er the
plains;

And the
mountains in
reply

Echoing
their joyous
strains.

A naked cherub is decently clothed with the addition of a paper streamer.

A luxurious lavender bow tops a host of smaller bows covering this tree.

The Space At The Base

After tumbling out of bed on Christmas morning, children wait impatiently to discover the gifts that have been left underneath the tree the night before. They look forward to seeing mountains of boxes in myriad shapes waiting for ribbons and wrappings to be torn off, revealing long-fantasized contents.

With presents mounded underneath the tree, there is a feeling of holiday cheer and seasonal opulence. However, once the packages have been opened and gifts removed, the base and stand come into view and remain visible until you dismantle the tree sometime shortly after New Year's Day. Yet there are many ways to make the area at the base of the tree as beautiful and engaging as the tree itself while allowing space for presents to be piled next to or nearby the base or underneath the tree.

Before decorating your tree, consider following this tip to reduce the mess caused by removing a tree when the holidays are over. Get a heavy-duty, plastic trash bag (the kind used for yard work), which is as deep as possible and wide enough to fit around the girth of the tree. Open the bag, place it on the floor where the tree will be set, and set the tree stand inside. Roll or fold the bag around the stand and conceal it with decorations or gift packages placed at the base of the tree.

When you are ready to take the tree out of the house, remove the stand from the tree base and unroll the bag up around the tree to encase it. Not only will the bag catch shedding needles, but it will protect the floor from water spilled when filling the tree stand.

Arrangements underneath the tree—like decorations for the tree itself or for other parts of your home—can be beautiful, light-hearted, and fanciful, ranging from creatively wrapped gifts to a collection of hats. The possibilities will be determined by the space available beneath the tree, which will depend on the kind of tree you select and on the height of the stand that holds it.

Plants
Some of the most attractive ideas are the simplest. If height permits, group pots of red and/or yellow poinsettias underneath the tree, making sure you use saucers to prevent moisture from damaging carpet or floor. Or, instead of poinsettias, choose a flowering plant or fragrant herb native to your area or a plant that you cultivate in your own garden. The most economical decorations consist of those items you already have in your home or that can be made from materials you have on hand.

Fabric
White fabric is often placed beneath a Christmas tree to hide the stand, to provide a surface on which to place presents, and to suggest snow. An old sheet might suffice, but a lace tablecloth, or a length of colorful or patterned fabric provides a handsome alternative.

Toys
Traditional ideas for the base of the Christmas tree include groupings of antique dolls, stuffed animals, and other toys—all of which impart a pleasant feeling of warmth and nostalgia. Combine a variety of toys, or select one or two kinds—old trucks and cars, or dolls dressed in the same-colored costumes or their Christmas best.

Collections
Consider your hobbies and interests and those of your family members. Are you a pack rat? Maybe you have an assortment of colorfully patterned and variously shaped cookie tins at the back of a kitchen cabinet. Put ribbons on them and place them under the tree. Do you have a collection of old glass bottles with unusual imprints? Tie bows around the necks and place the bottles beneath the tree where they will sparkle with reflections of the tree lights. Fond of old books? Arrange volumes of Christmas-related stories and revive the tradition of reading aloud every night.

Cushions
If you want to be original and love to sew, try an arrangement of small needlepoint, quilted, or embroidered pillows in a variety of shapes.

Wrapped Boxes
Wrap empty boxes with fabric (fabric is more durable than paper) to use as props year after year. Collect a wide variety of shapes including tubes and cylinders.

Nativity Scenes
A Nativity scene appropriately sized and scaled, containing both animals and figures, can also be set up underneath a tree. Or select props and assemble them into a theatrical set that tells the story of Rudolph, the red-nosed reindeer, or a family story.

Ornaments
If your family loves and plays music and your tree has a musical motif, place actual instruments, music boxes, and books of music scores at the base of the tree.

Baskets
Actual presents can be placed inside other, larger containers, such as baskets of various sizes. If the baskets have handles or are loosely woven, wrap or weave colorful ribbons and streamers through the holes. When the presents are opened, the baskets can remain as decorations that complement the tree.

A group of dainty porcelain-headed dolls protect their tree, at the same time obscuring the base.

CHAPTER 4

Deck The Halls

Make your home burst with color, joy, and goodwill

In addition to the tree, a myriad of decorations brightens homes during Christmas. Some, or their precursors, have heralded the holidays for centuries. Some originated in regions of America, but most come from other countries. There are traditional decorations, individual interpretations of old themes, and some original ideas. Although many are available ready-made, you and your family can make most of them at home.

This chapter shows many easy and beautiful decorations, offers ideas for using them, and gives directions for making them. Among the items are a number especially suitable for children to make or to help make. Many of these projects are for holiday ornaments for your own home but they can also serve as presents that convey special affection.

Possibilities for Christmas decorations are nearly limitless. Those described and pictured on the following pages may appeal to you and inspire you to create imaginative interpretations or altogether original ideas.

Evergreen garlands can be looped from newel posts, preceding page, draped over a mantel, left, or wrapped around balusters, opposite page.

Wreathed Greenery

reaths, like Christmas trees, are a part of the ancient tradition of bringing evergreens indoors around the time of the winter solstice as a symbol of life. In pre-Christian times, people in Egypt, the Mideast, the Orient, and Europe made wreaths from evergreens, herbs, and other materials. In decorating for the Saturnalia, ancient Romans always hung wreaths.

Christmas wreaths are usually thought of as hanging on doors, windows, or walls. Remember that evergreen wreaths may also lie flat. Table wreaths encircling candles create a delightful effect although you must be mindful of the potential fire danger — particularly with greenery that has begun to dry out.

Suspended from entry doors, walls, and windows or above mantels, or lying flat as centerpieces and table decorations, evergreen wreaths with berries, red ribbon, and perhaps cones, are one of the emblems of Christmas. They are attractive in every style of interior, and those made of coniferous foliage bring fresh outdoor fragrances inside.

At the grocery store you can find handsome embellishments for wreaths, including fruit, red chile peppers, small onions, heads of garlic, or radishes, all of which convey an impression of vitality and plenty. Other possible embellishments are pinecones and found natural objects such as seashells, dried fungus, seedpods, and nuts. Gold, silver, or colored glass balls or other Christmas tree ornaments can also be used. Fresh flowers (in a water-saturated

Right: Bunches of greenery are wired to a form.
Opposite page: The symmetry of the architecture was observed when decorating the doorway.

foam base or in concealed tubes of water) or artificial blooms provide additional shapes and colors. Don't overlook the possibilities of candies and cookies.

Then there is the traditional but not mandatory bow. Consider using several small bows instead of a single large one, or ribbon wound around the wreath, with or without a bow, or ribbon in colors other than red. As another variation, raffia can be wound around a wreath.

Legendary Evergreens

In selecting or making evergreen wreaths, you might take special pleasure in using those evergreens linked by custom and legend to Christmas or to even more ancient celebrations.

Fir: (*Tannenbaum* in German) was brought indoors by German tribes, probably far back into prehistory, to celebrate the winter solstice. It was also central to the early Christian legend from Germany about St. Boniface (see page 26).

Rosemary: an ancient symbol of remembrance, was used in medieval England to garnish the boar's head at the traditional Christmas feast. Legend holds that the tiny blossoms of rosemary changed forever from white to blue after the Virgin Mary hung the clothes of the infant Jesus (her own blue cloak in one version) on a rosemary bush to dry during the flight of the holy family to Egypt.

Holly: was for many ancient European peoples a protective plant that repelled witches, lightning, and poison. The Druids ascribed curative powers to it. Associated with the Crucifixion, its red berries and spring leaves became symbols of Christ's suffering. In Scandinavian countries holly was known as Christthorn. In the old English Christmas carol "The Holly and the Ivy," the tiny white flowers borne by the holly tree represent Mary, who bore Jesus, and the red berries represent Christ's blood. According to a German legend, if smooth, thornless holly was

The mistletoe
hung
in the
castle hall,

The holly
branch shone
on the
old oak wall.

Thomas Haynes Bayly
The Mistletoe Bough

Laying a wreath flat on a table and embellishing it with candles, above, is just as effective as the more usual tradition of hanging a wreath above a fireplace, opposite page.

brought indoors for Christmas, the wife would rule the household in the coming year, and the husband would rule if the leaves were thorny. Another belief held that holly decorations left up after New Year's Day brought bad luck.

Ivy: was associated with Bacchus, the Greek god of wine, and many legends that developed through the years link ivy and drink. One belief holds that ivy berries swallowed before wine is drunk will prevent intoxication—a quaint but inefficacious and dangerous remedy.

Ivy also became a symbol of love and in the Middle Ages was established as a customary Christmas decoration. In England, ivy was thought of as feminine, holly as masculine, perhaps explaining the carol "The Holly and the Ivy."

Mistletoe: a parasitic evergreen with white berries, was known throughout historic time in Europe as the golden bough. It has long been credited with many magical properties. According to folklore, these properties are most powerful at the solstices and the equinoxes.

In his famous study of mythology, magic, and religion, *The Golden Bough*, Sir James George Frazer points out that in Europe mistletoe grows chiefly on oaks and that oaks are struck by lightning far more frequently than other trees. Therefore, it is not surprising that various myths link mistletoe with gods that come down to earth in the form of lightning striking oak. Other myths have associated mistletoe with the sun and celestial fire.

As the Roman historian Pliny noted, the Druids worshiped mistletoe as a magical healer. Even in the twentieth century in places as scattered as Cambodia, Japan, and part of Africa, it has continued to be revered as a sacred healer.

Another widely claimed property of mistletoe is its ability to offer protection from witchcraft and sorcery. The Druids gathered it with golden sickles and never allowed this heaven-sent plant to touch the ground. Over much of the world, it is gathered differently from other plants and shown special respect. The Church condemned it for centuries as evil and pagan. Finally, however, in some countries mistletoe was incorporated into a Christmas ritual in which a holy kiss of peace and pardon was initiated by the priest and passed through the congregation. This probably explains the origin of kissing under the mistletoe.

Another possible historic source of this custom is the placement of mistletoe on the high altar of York Cathedral at Christmas as part of a proclamation of universal liberty. One liberty quickly established as custom was the right of men to kiss any woman found standing under the mistletoe.

No rule holds you to choosing traditional Christmas evergreens to make wreaths. For variety or practicality, consider those that are readily available. For example, you might use the lower limbs trimmed from the Christmas tree. Perhaps your garden offers supplies.

Gardens and shops sometimes have foliage from southern magnolia, boxwood, arborvitae, yew, hemlock, eucalyptus, leucothoe, cryptomeria, incense cedar, Grecian laurel, California bay laurel, and mahonia. Make the most of the various kinds of greenery available to you. Notice how contrasts among bright, dark, bluish, or grayish, and glossy or flat greens create variety and visual interest. Similarly, differences in sizes of foliage can be used to make attractive wreaths. Also consider artificial wreaths and loose artificial greenery, which are practical for their permanence and fire safety.

Red berries are the most common complement to greenery in wreaths. Red or near red berries widely available at Christmas include those of holly, cotoneaster, pyracantha, hawthorn, rose, wintercreeper,

strawberry tree, toyon, nandina, yew, Natal plum, honeysuckle, and bittersweet. Berries of some plants such as nandina shed less easily if the stems are dipped in shellac thinned with rubbing alcohol or in liquid wax.

Herbal Wreaths

Possibilities for Christmas wreaths extend well beyond using the traditional evergreens.

Herbal wreaths are an ancient form of Christmas decoration. Fragrant and muted in color, they are made with either fresh or dried herbs, or a combination of the two. Herbs can be used alone or mixed with other plant materials such as geranium leaves, dried flowers, seedpods, or berries.

Living Wreaths

Because of their varied colors, textures, and growth habits, and their capacity to endure more dryness than most plants, several kinds of succulents make handsome wreaths. Rosettes of hen and chicks (*Echeveria*) and smaller sedums, including burro's tail (*S. morganianum*), offer a fascinating diversity in size and shape. Small ivies, such as those recommended above, make excellent coverings for topiary frames. Some of the smaller bromeliads—diminutive tillandsia and cryptanthus—contribute starry forms, varied textures, and unusual colors. As filler, try a tiny ground cover such as moss basket ivy (*Cymbalaria*), Scotch or Irish moss (*Sagina*), baby's tears (*Soleirolia*), creeping thyme (*Thymus*), or Australian violet (*Viola hederacea*). Rapidly growing plants that quickly become spindly or that point upward are unsuitable for living wreaths.

A bay leaf wreath, above, will later be useful in the kitchen. Ornaments such as the nesting birds, left, can be wired to a form (see page 89).

The Story of the Holly Sprig

BY ARTHUR UPSON

"I 'd be the shiniest green,"
 Wished once a sprig of holly,
"That e'er at Yule was seen,
 And deck some banquet jolly!"

"I 'd be the cheeriest red,"
 Wished once the holly-berry,
"That e'er at board rich spread
 Helped make the feasters merry!"

The life within them heard
 Down dark and silent courses,
For each wish is a word
 To those fair-hidden sources.

All Summer in the wood,
 While they were riper growing,
The deep roots understood,
 And helped without their knowing.

In a little market stall
 At Yule the sprig lay waiting,
For fine folk one and all
 Passed by that open grating.

The Eve of Christmas Day
 It had been passed by many,
When one turned not away
 And bought it for a penny.

Hers was a home of care
 Which not a wreath made jolly;
The only Christmas there
 Was that sweet sprig of holly.

"Oh, this is better far
 Than banquet!" thought the berry;
The leaves glowed like a star
 And made that cottage merry!

From St. Nicholas Magazine, c. 1907.

Don't feel restricted to displaying just one wreath. This collection hung in a window is enjoyed from inside and out.

Making Wreaths

Many different materials and methods can be employed to make evergreen wreaths.

Soldered wire frames are sold by florists, floral-supply companies, and hobby shops in several sizes and types. Greenery and other materials may be wired directly to the frames, or the curved troughs of the most elaborate type can be packed with sphagnum, Spanish, or excelsior, in order to provide a base into which evergreens and ornaments may be inserted. To keep the moss in place, wrap clear nylon fishing line around the covered frame.

You can make a simple frame by shaping a heavy wire such as a coat hanger, or multiple loops of wire, into a hoop and wrapping the hoop with floral tape. Forms made out of straw, vine or willow stems, excelsior, plastic foam, and floral-foam are all alternatives to wire frames.

When making a hanging wreath, take a tip from the professionals: Suspend the frame on a door or an easel when attaching greenery and other materials. This way you can more easily see how the wreath will look when in place.

Floral picks are useful for making "stems" for leaves so that they may be more easily bound to a frame. Picks also create longer, more manageable stems. Wire stems securely to picks, then cover the wire by wrapping the pick with floral tape.

Basic Evergreen Wreath

This version is essentially traditional, but you can substitute many other materials and improvise on the design by adding individual touches. This wreath is suitable for a front door or an inside wall.

The materials you need will depend on the size of the wreath you wish to make, the form you decide to use, and the foliage you wrap around the form. Therefore, the following list should be used as a guide only.

Bare stems flexible enough to
  bend into a ring,
  or a foam shape,
  or a double-wire frame
Pliers
Sprigs of foliage,
  including lots of tips
Spool of 22-gauge green
  floral wire
Wire cutters
Ribbon (optional)
Liquid glue
Decorations of your choice

If the base will be made out of bare stems, soak them in water until they can be bent into a circle without snapping. Make thick sections more pliable by breaking the fibers with a pair of pliers.

Condition evergreen foliage by trimming stem ends and immersing foliage overnight in tepid water. Make bunches of foliage about 6 inches long.

These bunches will be tied onto the base so that cut ends of stem segments are always concealed and growing tips are at tops of bunches. Therefore, use as many sprigs as necessary to make bunches that will result in a full, attractive wreath.

1. Holding several lengths of soaked stems in a bunch, bend them to form a circle.

2. Position a bunch of foliage onto the base and wire it firmly in place.

3. Moving in either direction, wire bunches onto frame so that the tips cover the stems of the preceding bunch.

4. Fluff out the bunches and, if necessary, add bunches to inner, outer, and center parts to completely cover the frame.

5. Turn over the wrapped base and attach a wire or ribbon hanger to the base.

6. Dip decorations into liquid glue and position them. Or, wire decorations to the base.

I will honor
Christmas
in my
heart, and try
to keep
it all the year.

Charles Dickens
A Christmas Carol, 1843

*Snow falls around a glass-
enclosed tree when
you shake this collectible.*

*Tchaikovsky's Nutcracker
Suite is responsible for wooden
soldiers doing a tour
of duty at Christmastime.*

Collections

The main reason for decorating the house during the Christmas season is to make your home look as festive and inviting as possible to the many guests and family members who will visit. Certain decorations are traditionally considered part of the Christmas celebration and more than likely you have these carefully packed in boxes that are brought out every year. However, there is no reason why you cannot take this opportunity to display treasures that—up until now—have had no real seasonal significance.

Grouping similar objects is a strategy used often by interior designers: One throw cushion can get lost on a settee, but a group adds color and decorative impact. The same is true of prints on a wall or ornaments in a

90

bookcase. Try this approach with your Christmas decorations, too.

The fact that your collection makes a decorative impact is reason enough to exhibit it, but you can also attach special meaning to the display and make it a unique part of your family's memories of Christmas at home. An international collection of dolls, for example, might symbolize families around the world celebrating the same holiday with the same spirit and goodwill. Or a display of photographs of your entire family could emphasize togetherness, whether or not everyone pictured is able to attend your celebrations. A grouping of antique toys can remind everyone that giving gifts to children has been a Christmas tradition for hundreds of years. A collection of nutcrackers or molds can signify that Christmas is a time for feasting and plentiful food. A gleaming group of well-polished silver candlesticks can symbolize the light that shines on all of us. A collection of china, glass, or wooden animals might suggest that people and animals must peacefully share this planet with each other.

With a little thought you can find some Christmas meaning in almost anything you wish to display. You can make your collection even more appropriate by adding Christmas finery. A group of dolls, for example, can be dressed up in Christmas outfits. Or you can enhance a grouping of nutcrackers with a basket full of nuts or cookie cutters with a tray laden with decorated cookies. And any display can be enlivened and made suitable for the season with the addition of evergreen boughs, holly sprigs, silver balls, and colorful ribbons. The impact of your collection can be strengthened by continuing the theme on and around the tree.

If you don't have a collection that you feel is worthy of display, maybe this year is the time to start one—and start a tradition, as well. Decide on a theme, add it to your Christmas list, or let it be known to anyone who will be buying you a gift that you are starting a particular collection. If the gift buyer knows that the gift recipient would welcome, for example, any piece of blue and white china or any kind of wooden kitchen utensil, Christmas shopping becomes easy and a pleasure. And for the recipients, the fact that their collection has been formed or enlarged through the generosity of others adds special meaning to each object.

Above: Make a special outfit for a treasured heirloom. Dress her and sit her in a chair where she can act as chaperone of the party.
Left: Clear out a cupboard in honor of the holidays and use the empty shelves on which to set up Christmas scenes.

Christmas Scenes

With a few figures of wood, glass, ceramic, or other materials, you can set up a tabletop scene and establish a Christmas tradition in your home. Over the years, as the same figures are brought out and set up at Christmas, they will acquire more and more meaning. An important part of this custom is a sense of continuity, for you and perhaps for generations to come. That sense of continuity helps to explain the magic of Christmas in the home.

Crèches

Legend ascribes the invention of the Nativity scene, often called by its French name, crèche (literally manger or crib), to St. Francis of Assisi. According to the legend, near the village of Greccio he created a large outdoor presepe (the Italian name) to provide a setting for the reenactment of the Nativity, complete with hay, manger, and live ox, burro, and people. This scene had actually been created earlier by the clergy in their mystery plays (see page 26).

St. Francis' example did, however, revive the custom of making a crèche. In little time elaborate versions appeared in a variety of settings over most of Europe. In Catholic countries the popularity of the crèche has never waned. Crèches were originally, and have remained, largely public displays—living tableaux, or even technologically up-to-date versions with mechanical gears and sophisticated electrical lighting.

Even in predominantly Protestant countries, the crèche has survived, for example, in miniature form as an adornment on elaborate kissing balls. Over much of Europe, wherever the Christmas pyramid came to be used, crèches were arranged on the lowest shelves. The custom of setting up crèches, large or small, came to the New World and, over both Americas, has produced many charming styles and variations.

In the United States, one of the more delightful crèche traditions

Any flat surface can display a village of lit houses, above, a group of angels, opposite page above, or a church choir, opposite page below. Make sure the crèches are safely out of the reach of small fingers.

was established by Moravian settlers. In Bethlehem, Pennsylvania, an extravagant crèche (or *putz*, as the Moravians called it) includes dozens of Christmas trees as well as the usual figures and trappings. Public displays, in churchyards, parks and squares, but also on private property, have become popular. Small-scale crèches in the home—on a tabletop or mantel, or beneath the Christmas tree, for example—are also common. Every holiday season, when the small figures and structures are unpacked, they are often as significant as the Christmas tree.

Tableaux

In addition to the crèche, there are many other tableaux that you can create to represent the spirit of Christmas. Depictions of a choir of angels, a menagerie, or a street or village can make charming additions to your Christmas decorations. The more personal the scene, the more enjoyable and meaningful it will be to you and your family.

A tableau is an ideal project to turn over to children. They can comb through toy boxes to find appropriate elements or use building sets to make their own. And, if they are stumped, there are many inspiring books available that have pages of houses and ornaments designed to be cut out, folded, and glued. Alternatively, supply them with magazines containing pictures they can cut out and glue to cardboard stands.

Use your ingenuity to make or embellish these scenes. White sand or soap flakes can look like snow and small sprigs of nipped off pine boughs can serve as miniature trees.

Pictured here are some examples of tableaux that can be set on a mantel, coffee table, or buffet. The center of the dining table or a shelf in a bookcase or hutch are other good locations for a Christmas scene. Any flat-topped surface is a potential stage as long as it is out of the reach of small fingers or wagging tails.

The tradition of kissing under the mistletoe probably stems from the ancient belief that this vine offers protection from witchcraft and sorcery.

The Kissing Ball

Far more ancient than the Christmas tree is the kissing ball, also called kissing bough, kissing bunch, or kissing ring. It has long decorated houses in England and in Germany, where it is called the *Küssenbaum*. The main component is mistletoe.

According to tradition, the presence of mistletoe was license for any man or boy to kiss the maid of his choice. Although the actual origin of this merry custom is unclear, some claim that it is due to the belief that mistletoe offers protection from witchcraft and sorcery. The Druids gathered it with golden sickles and never allowed this "heaven-sent" plant to touch the ground. Over much of the world, it is gathered differently from other plants and shown special respect. (For more on the folklore surrounding mistletoe, see page 84.)

Nowadays, a mere sprig of mistletoe hanging in a doorway is excuse enough for anyone passing beneath to kiss or be kissed. However, if you wish to be more true to tradition, consider making a kissing ball.

The traditional English kissing ball, which hangs from the ceiling, is a sphere or a crown of evergreens, candles, and seven apples framing the mistletoe. Variations on this basic form came to be ornamental, like the Christmas tree, with small animal figures, paper ornaments, tinsel, ribbon, stars, and crèches. In former times carols were sung beneath the kissing ball, and other Christmas rituals were performed there. In some remote rural areas of England, even into the twentieth century, Christmas trees were apparently unknown and presents were hung from a kissing ball. For many centuries in England the kissing ball was the center of Christmas in the home, just as the Christmas tree is over much of the world today.

The following directions and suggestions are for making two versions of the kissing ball. You can use these, vary them—for example, omit the apples—or simply make a sphere of mistletoe with a bow on top and ribbon streamers beneath it.

In the English Tradition

Of the two traditional forms, the crown (or half-sphere) and the sphere, the latter is probably seen more often today. The outermost part is a sphere of evergreen attached to a specially shaped frame. The kissing ball is topped by a bow, has a bunch of mistletoe hanging from the bottom, and is ringed with candles. One candle is placed at the bottom of the sphere. Suspended inside are seven apples (or six apples and a silver ball), which are said to have originally represented positions of the sun around the earth.

The candles and drying evergreen create a potential fire hazard. Plan either to use the candles unlit or to burn them briefly, perhaps as the traditional ritual lighting at a New Year's Eve gathering. If the candles are to be burned, place them so the flames will be far away from foliage or other flammable materials, and be sure that foliage is fresh and moist. Turn the page for step-by-step directions on how to make a safer version of a traditional kissing ball.

"Under the Mistletoe," from an engraving dated 1868.

How to Make a Kissing Ball

This Kissing Ball, like traditional versions, takes the form of a sphere and includes mistletoe and trailing ribbons. Artificial foliage, berries, and flowers are nontraditional decorations that add color and shape. Follow the directions given or try variations. Mistletoe is an essential ingredient but any type of foliage, flowers, or ornament could be added.

You can make this Christmas decoration out of any materials you have on hand. Use the following list as a guide.

Artificial mistletoe, holly, or ivy greens; red berries; edelweiss flowers; or other plants and foliage
Floral wire
Wire cutters
Floral tape
Scissors
4 yards ribbon (¼″–½″ wide)
1 wood embroidery hoop (7″–10″ dia, 2 pieces)

1. Assemble all the tools and materials you'll need. Separate greens into individual pieces and, if necessary, lengthen stems with floral wire covered with floral tape.

2. Cut off 1½ yards of ribbon and, allowing 6 inches to 12 inches for trailing ends, wind it tightly around the smaller of the two embroidery hoops.

3. When the hoop is completely covered, securely tie both ends and allow them to trail. Wind and tie ribbon around the larger hoop in the same manner, making sure the tightening screw is left uncovered.

4. Insert smaller hoop inside larger hoop, rotating and centering them to form a sphere. When you are satisfied with the shape, tighten screw in larger hoop. Wrap points where hoops intersect with floral wire to secure in place.

5. Bend stems or wire-lengthened stems of artificial mistletoe into long hooks. Repeat with other greens and flower stems, varying length of each sprig and making sure that mistletoe sprig is the longest.

6. Attach greenery to sphere by hooking bent stems around hoops. Secure with floral wire. Start with longest sprig, layer the rest placing shortest sprigs closest to the hoops.

7. Finish Kissing Ball by filling in sphere with additional sprigs of mistletoe and clusters of red berries and leaves, adjusted to cover exposed joints and wires. Attach a small cluster at top joint, adding a length of ribbon or nylon filament to use as a hanger. Tie on extra lengths of trailing ribbon, if desired.

As long as it contains mistletoe, a kissing ball can be fashioned out of your choice of additional materials. This one includes artificial edelweiss.

The Yule Log

All over Europe, lighting the Yule log on Christmas Eve has been a tradition for centuries. The Yule log predates Christianity, going back to the Vikings and, still further, to prehistoric times, when most Europeans lived as forest-dwelling tribes. In France the *Bûche de Noël* is still lighted in some homes on Christmas Eve; in England, it is the Christmas or Yule log that is lighted; in Italy, it is called the *ceppo*. From Italy, Spain, Greece, and Bulgaria to Scandinavia, a log is lighted in the home on Christmas Eve.

Over many centuries a complex of legend and myth has developed around all versions of this custom. English colonists brought to America the custom of the Yule log with the lore that surrounded it.

Common to early Scandinavian custom and corresponding customs in other countries was the belief that lighting the log represented the triumph of light over darkness and the rebirth of the sun. In Scandinavia the custom also honored Thor, god of thunder and protector of the human race from evil demons. Lighting the log generally became a symbolic repelling of evil, and signified an assurance of good crops and fertility of both people and livestock. Throughout Europe the custom came to be a part of joyous celebration, with feasting, drinking, and singing. In many countries the log is part of a ritual bestowing of gifts.

The most common trees used for Yule logs are ash, oak, beech, and pine. Decoration of the log has been traditional in many countries. Over the centuries, sprigs of evergreens were a widely used decoration. In England, Yule logs were often dragged to the fireplaces of great halls with ivy-covered ropes.

If you have a fireplace, even a small one, consider putting a decorated Yule log into it early in the Christmas season and burning the log on Christmas Eve. Provide a magical link with Christmases past to warm your home and provide a focus for fellowship and good cheer.

Whether your fireplace is a working one or not, tradition demands that you display a Yule log in the hearth at Christmastime.

Heap on more
wood!—the wind
is chill;

But let
it whistle as
it will,

We'll keep our
Christmas
merry still.

Sir Walter Scott
"The Lay of the Last Minstrel"

Decorating a Log

The simplest and most usual decoration for a Yule log is a wide ribbon tied into a large bow. However, if you have the time and the desire, the decorations can be more lavish.

If you plan on lighting a fire before Christmas Eve, it makes sense to set the Yule log beside, rather than in, the fireplace. It will look attractive sitting on the hearth and wrapped with a garland. Or you can drill holes into the log and tuck in ornaments, bows, or sprigs of holly or greenery.

If you prefer, cradle the log in a large basket lined with a bed of pinecones, sweet-smelling wood chips, colorful tissue paper, or any other material that evokes the spirit of Christmas. If the basket is loosely

A Yule log is only special once it is brought inside and decorated. Before then it is merely firewood from the barn.

woven, you can weave ribbon through the holes and the handle.

Before lighting the log, be sure to remove any decorations that could flare up dangerously or melt and give off toxic fumes.

There is no reason to limit yourself to a single Yule log. You could build a tower of logs into a conical pile resembling a Christmas tree and make a ritual out of burning one log each night when you open a door on the Advent calendar. The last (and largest) log would be the one that is burned on Christmas Eve.

Garlands and Plaques

Garlands, also swags or sprays, consist of several evergreen branches wired together and hung. Anywhere a wreath might be used, a garland is also appropriate. Garlands can also decorate places too narrow for wreaths, such as newel posts and spaces between windows. Plaques are similar in appearance to garlands, but the solid backing allows heavier, more elaborate ornamentation, as with fruit. Plaques are hung on doors or walls—always against flat, firm surfaces. Both plaques and garlands are yet other forms of evergreen decorations that have enlivened homes in early winter for centuries.

Use available materials to create garlands or plaques that suit your tastes and express your creativity.

Simple Garland

Simplest of evergreen Christmas decorations, a garland is also the easiest and quickest to make. You can add to or alter this basic design.

Rope or wire, for spines
Dark green floral tape
Evergreen branches or
*   stems of flame-retardant*
*   artificial pine*
Spool of 16- or 18-gauge
*   floral wire*
Satin ribbon in desired color

1. Make spines out of appropriate lengths of rope or wire. Wrap with floral tape.
2. Wire evergreen branches onto individual spines.

Like well-plucked eyebrows,
the swags topping the
windows add to the groomed
look of this dining room
that lacks nothing
except the dinner guests.

3. Shape tops of spines into loops so that the garland can be hung on door or wall from tacks or hooks.
4. Hang or attach bows and streamers after garlands have been installed.

Country Plaque

Excellent for a front door, this decoration suggests the holiday season as well as the agricultural bounty of the region where it is made. A decoration need not be regional, but if you want to make a plaque appropriate to your area, consider the range of natural materials, from vegetables to seashells and dry weeds, that are at hand.

2-inch-thick plastic foam
Moss or tree lichen
Fern and moss pins
Dark green spray paint (optional)
Sprigs of evergreen
Spool of 16- or 18-gauge
*   floral wire*
Floral picks, large and small
Decorations such as small
*   artichokes, tangerines or*
*   mandarin oranges, walnuts,*
*   chile peppers, dried gourds,*
*   kumquats, sprays of California*
*   pepper berries, bunches of toyon*
*   or madrone berries, dried*
*   teasel flowers*

1. Cut a piece of foam the size and shape desired. Cover with moss held by fern pins, or spray the foam with green paint.
2. Wire individual sprigs of evergreen onto floral picks, and insert around edges of foam slab. Use longer sprigs at bottom.
3. Attach decorations to pieces of wire or to floral picks and decorate the plaque as desired. Fill in any gaps with extra evergreen sprigs.

It is not until you look around that you realize how many features there are in a home that would be even more attractive when decked out in greenery. For example, a stair rail, opposite page, is draped with branches tied with ribbon to the banister. After the garland is in place, you can add extra decorations such as a few pieces of wheat, some sprigs of real or artificial flowers, and the occasional decoration to provide glitter. A music stand, above, is used to display sprigs of green as well as an appropriate score. The entrance into a Victorian-style living room, left, is accented with a long garland. Garlands of evergreens are also wrapped around the wire that suspends paintings from the picture rail.

Because Christmas is so
close to
Thanksgiving—a time to
give thanks for
Nature's bounty—adding
fruit and flowers to
an evergreen garland is a
suitable touch. And
because the
hearth is the natural place
for family gatherings,
this is the
appropriate place to make
your statement.
Place heavier items, such
as the fruit in the
garland, right, where they
will be supported on
the mantel.
Decorate the portions that
hang down on either
side with sprays
of dried flowers. Evergreen
garlands join the
gesso ones attached to the
ornate mirror,
below. Leaf rosettes define
the corners of the
fireplace, opposite page.
Paying further
homage to Thanksgiving,
an apple cone sits in
the center of a
fireside dining table.

104

Flower Arrangements

Fresh, colorful flower arrangements are glorious additions at any time of the year. During the Christmas season, they help to warm the winter gloom that seeps inside like a chilling draft from the outdoors. Bright red tulips, white narcissus, or any available cut or container-grown flowers bring Christmas vitality into a room.

Preparation and Care

To keep cut flowers looking their best in a vase for as long as possible, buy only the freshest flowers, ensure that their tissues have a generous, accessible supply of water and nutrients, and place the flowers where they will be least affected by heat and dryness. Give thought to your choice of flowers, bearing in mind that an arrangement looks fresh no longer than the life of its least durable specimen.

Find a florist who dependably stocks fresh blossoms in clear, unclouded water, even though prices may be higher than in bargain shops. Select stems that are firm and crisp, not limp, with blossoms that are newly opened, or just beginning to open. If the outdoor temperature is below freezing when you take flowers out of the shop, protect them from prolonged exposure to outside air as well as parching blasts from the car heater. Keep them out of water for the shortest possible time.

At home, place stem ends in a large open container—a clean sink or dishpan will do—and with a sharp, clean blade remove at least an inch of each stem. Make the cut under water in order to prevent air bubbles from entering and blocking the vascular system, which conducts water to the flowers. If flowers need to be conditioned, transfer them directly to a deep, well-scrubbed container of clean, tepid (110° F) water, and allow them to remain overnight, or several

hours at least, with stems and foliage, but not blossoms, completely submerged. (Fuzzy leaves, however, will become soggy if submerged for very long.) This conditioning process will amply reward your efforts with long-lasting flowers.

After conditioning and before arranging flowers, recut stems under water and remove all leaves that would be beneath the water level of the vase. Arrange flowers in a clean vase, using fresh floral foam, clean pin holders, or wire netting, if needed, and clean water containing additives, as discussed on page 108.

Throughout the above discussion, the emphasis is on cleanliness—clean water, clean cutting implements, clean containers. Cleanliness is imperative for a very practical reason: Given the opportunity, bacteria

Above: For a dinner party, decorate the buffet with tissue-wrapped bunches of flowers. At the end of the evening, present each guest with a bouquet. Opposite page: Colorful poinsettia bracts are tucked into a string of evergreen magnolia leaves on the mantel. An elaborate floral decoration is set in front of a nonworking fireplace.

Above: Banked above a display of flower-covered cushions is a bouquet that includes branches of variegated holly leaves. Opposite page: The wreath, corsage, boutonniere, and nosegay are designed for a Christmas wedding. Fruit and greenery are combined with narcissus, stephanotis, lily of the valley, chincherinchee, freesia, and tulip.

proliferate in vase water and promote decay in cut stem ends, blocking upward flow of water. Because bruised tissue makes a breeding place for bacteria, it is more effective to split woody stem ends rather than hammer them to a pulp.

In addition to practicing good hygiene to prevent or slow bacterial growth, you can use a commercial floral additive containing one or more ingredients that retard bacterial growth in vase water. Or, you can add ¼ teaspoon of liquid bleach per gallon of water or the same amount of powdered citric acid per gallon of water. Commercial additives contain sugar that feeds plant tissues, extends vase life of flowers, and encourages buds to open. If you prefer, make your own preservative by mixing 1 tablespoon of granulated sugar in a gallon of water that also contains bleach or citric acid.

To preserve the freshness of an arrangement for as long as possible, place it in a cool spot away from

warm sunlight, open fire, and heating ducts. Avoid the warm top of a television. Moving a vase of flowers to the floor during the night can prolong its life by keeping it cool.

Above all, check water level in vase often and keep vase filled. An arrangement, particularly in a warm room, transpires—like a Christmas tree—at a surprising rate.

Clever Imitations

Virtually all of the functions of cut flowers can be filled—beautifully and without worry about freshness and vase life—by artificial flowers.

If you recoil at the image of garishness and obvious fakery that the thought of artifical flowers generally conjures, take a look at the best (and usually costliest) of them. Most common are the silks, the finest of which are hard to distinguish, even at close range, from the blossoms and foliage that they imitate. (The cheapest silks, on the other hand, confirm prejudices against artificial flowers.)

Cotton flowers can be equally convincing. The best silk and cotton blossoms are often skillfully contoured and handpainted, so that, for example, a typical 'Peace' rose petal is shaded from gold tones at its base to palest pink and to rich rosy pink at its outer edges. Only the scent is missing. One of the most delightful and realistic of the artificial flowers is a Southern magnolia made of silk and suede. The perfectly cupped, mat white petals are silk, and the leaves are suede in just the right shade of deep green, with convincing contours, subtly embossed veins, and fuzzy brown undersides. One or two stems, together with red candles, can create an attractive—and carefree— Christmas decoration in your home.

Leaves are also duplicated in artificial materials. These various kinds of artificial leaves and flowers, used singly, combined, or mixed with dried flowers, are practical, durable and, at their best, as lovely as the ephemeral plants that they imitate.

The container is as important as the flowers it holds. If it is appropriate it adds to the beauty of the arrangement. If inappropriate, it can ruin the effect. Hollowed-out logs, obscuring the water holders, make the tulips, left, almost look like they are growing in the woods.

Slender glass vases support the tall stems of dried grasses in an elegant arrangement, above. As holds true with most collections, a grouping of vases creates a more interesting display than individual arrangements. To link the vases into a cohesive group, a few pinecones are scattered on the shelf.

Dark green evergreen needles, below, are even lusher when contrasted with fresh tulips and arranged in a gleaming copper bowl.

Bulbs That Can Be Forced

Whichever kind of bulb you choose, be sure the variety you purchase is marked "good for forcing," especially if—as is the case with tulips, hyacinths, and daffodils—many varieties are available. It is wise to order your selections well in advance—in the spring if possible—to ensure their availability. Most bulb suppliers will deliver at the right time for planting in your area.

If you receive an early shipment or for some reason can't plant the bulbs immediately, store them in a cool (35° to 50° F) place. The refrigerator is ideal, but don't put them in the same crisper as ripe fruit. If they are packed in boxes or paper bags, open them up to provide ventilation. Bulbs can be stored this way for several weeks. Remember that bulbs are living plants. Handle them carefully and avoid freezing them.

Above and right: Amaryllis is a showy bloomer that generally makes its appearance at Christmastime. The 8- to 10-inch flowers can be red, pink, salmon, orange, or white. Opposite page: In their natural habitat, most bulbs will bloom in the spring. However, they can be forced to bloom indoors so that you can enjoy their springtime fragrance much earlier.

Forcing Bulbs

Add another dimension to Christmas floral displays with a show of vibrant flowering bulbs. Not only will your home be filled with the colors and scents of spring, you will have a ready supply of Christmas gifts that will always be welcome.

Stimulating a bulb to bloom out of season is known as forcing and is an easy and rewarding way to add freshness to your holiday decor. Bulbs commonly forced are narcissus, tulips, hyacinths, and crocuses. Others that can easily be forced include galanthuses, Dutch and reticulata irises, and grape hyacinths. Try experimenting with other hardy bulbs as well. (See page 115.)

Planting

Bulbs to be forced should be planted in mid to late September in order to bloom near Christmas. They require a cooling period of approximately 14 to 15 weeks.

The planting medium anchors the bulbs in place and holds moisture for rooting. Bulbs contain enough food for the developing flowers and shouldn't be fertilized during forcing. They must have excellent drainage or they will rot—but they shouldn't be allowed to dry out. Use clean pots that have drainage holes in the bottom. If you use clay pots, first soak them overnight so they won't draw moisture from the planting medium.

Fill each pot loosely with soil. The tops of the bulbs should be even with the rim when placed in the pot. Don't compress the soil or press the bulbs into it; the soil under the bulbs should remain loose so roots can grow easily through it. After the bulbs are in, fill the pots to the rim. The first watering will settle the soil enough to provide headspace for future watering. Water the pots two or three times to be absolutely sure all the soil is moist.

Plant about 3 hyacinths, 6 daffodils or tulips, or 15 crocuses in a 6-inch pot or bulb pan. When planting tulips, place the bulb so that the flat side faces toward the outside of the pot. The first large leaf of each plant will then face outward, creating a uniform appearance. As you plant each pot, label it with the name of the variety of the bulb, the planting date, and the date you intend to bring it indoors for forcing.

Cooling the Bulbs

All hardy bulbs need a period of cooling at temperatures between 35° and 50° F to prepare them for later leaf and flower growth.

Some bulbs, especially tulips that are sold in mild-climate regions, may have been partially "precooled" by the producer. These can be given the remainder of the 14 to 15 weeks of chilling that they require, then planted for forcing. If you hold bulbs in the refrigerator for more than 3 weeks, subtract 3 weeks from the required cooling time.

Cooling methods vary, but any structure where temperatures can be kept at 35° to 50° F can be used. Many people find a root cellar or an unheated basement the most convenient; others use an old refrigerator. During this apparently inactive cooling period, the roots are forming, so

Forced daffodils add color and cheer to a cold, wet December day.

the soil must be kept moist. Check the soil weekly.

In areas where the winter temperatures drop below zero, pots can be cooled in a trench in the garden or in a bulb frame or other cold frame. With either of these methods, it is important to keep the pots from freezing. A frame used for this purpose should be shaded and well drained. After the pots are placed in the frame, cover them with any loose insulating material, such as sand, sawdust, or straw.

If you choose to cool the bulbs in a trench, select a sloping location to aid in drainage. Dig a trench about 6 inches wider than the pots and deep enough for the pots to be below the frost line. Spread an inch of gravel or cinders on the bottom of the trench for drainage, and set the pots in the trench. Cover them with a few inches of sand, and finish filling the trench with soil.

Just before freezing weather, cover the trench with an insulating mulch. Bales of straw are convenient, and can be removed and replaced easily during the winter.

For a succession of blooms with either of these methods, place pots in storage in the reverse order in which you wish to remove them.

If there is any danger of mice burrowing into the mulch and damaging bulbs, top the trench with a ¼-inch-mesh wire screen before applying mulch. A diagram of where the pots are placed in the trench and which bulbs are in each pot will help you locate the one you want when you're ready to bring each pot indoors. If the weather is dry, be sure to water the pots frequently.

Forcing the Blooms

At the forcing stage, the pots are brought out of their cooled environment into warmth and light, triggering the formation of leaves and flowers. From the time the pots are removed from storage, they will require about three or four weeks to

bloom. If you wish bulbs to bloom for Christmas, bring them indoors around the end of November.

For best results, give the bulbs a temperature of 60° F and direct sunlight. Rotate the pots regularly so that all the leaves receive an equal amount of light. To prolong the bloom, remove the plants from direct sunlight when they begin to flower. Keep the soil moist throughout the forcing period.

If you're aiming for a specific flowering date and growth is occurring too quickly, blooming can be delayed by moving the pots to a cool (40° to 50° F) room out of direct sunlight (but not in darkness). Reaccustom them gradually to sunlight and warmer temperatures when you want them to resume growing.

After blooming, hardy bulbs cannot be forced again. A few, such as daffodils, can be transplanted into the garden in spring, but it will take them two or three years to reach their full blooming potential again. Most, such as tulips and hyacinths, are best discarded after forcing.

Forcing Without Soil

Hyacinths are sometimes forced in special "hyacinth glasses," shaped like an hourglass, with an upper compartment for the bulb and a lower compartment into which the roots grow. The bottom of the bulb should be just at water level in the lower section of the glass. Add water as needed to maintain this level during growth. Cool the bulb in its container for 14 to 15 weeks; then place it in bright light where daytime temperatures are 60° to 65° F. There are also tiny bottles available in which crocuses can be grown the same way. This unusual method of forcing enables you to watch the roots grow.

Forcing Without Cooling

The tender, paper-white narcissus (*Narcissus tazetta*), the yellow variety, 'Soleil d'Or', and the large bulbs of the Chinese sacred lily (*Narcissus tazetta orientalis*) can all be forced without cooling.

The usual—and very easy—way to grow them is to use an undrained, decorative bowl. First, fill the container with enough pebbles, gravel, coarse sand, pearl chips, or similar material to reach about 1 inch below the top of the bowl. Add water until it is barely below the surface of the gravel. Set the bulbs on top and hold them in place by adding enough gravel to cover approximately the bottom quarter of each bulb. Carefully maintain the water level.

An alternative method is to use vermiculite as a planting medium. Thoroughly saturate it; then gently squeeze out the excess moisture and place the vermiculite loosely in the container. Set the bulbs in place and partially cover them, leaving about three fourths of each bulb visible. The vermiculite should be kept evenly moist throughout the entire forcing process.

Tender narcissus are best kept in a cool (50° to 60° F) spot in low light until they are well-rooted and the shoots appear—usually about two to three weeks. They should then be placed in direct sunlight until they begin to flower, then moved into lower light. Because these bulbs cannot be forced again, after blooming they must be discarded.

Bulb Varieties for Forcing

Crocus
Flower Record (Purple)
Joan of Arc (White)
Large Yellow (Yellow)
Peter Pan (White)
Pickwick (Striped)
Purpureus
    grandiflorus (Purple)
Remembrance (Purple)
Victor Hugo (Purple)

Grape Hyacinth
Early Giant (Blue)

Hyacinth
Amethyst (Violet)
Amsterdam (Pink)
Anne Marie (Pink)
Bismarck (Blue)
Blue Jacket (Blue)
Carnegie (White)
Colosseum (White)
Delft Blue (Blue)
Jan Bos (Red)
L'Innocence (White)
Lady Derby (Pink)
Marconi (Pink)
Marle (Blue)
Ostara (Blue)
Pink Pearl (Pink)

Iris
Danfordiae (Yellow)
Harmony (Blue)
Hercules (Purple)

Narcissus
Barrett Browning (Orange
    and white)
Carlton (Yellow)
Chinese Sacred Lily (White)
Dutch Master (Yellow)
Fortune (Bicolor)
Ice Follies (Cream and white)
Joseph MacLeod (Yellow)
Magnet (Yellow and white)
Mt. Hood (White)
Paper-white (White)
Soleil d'Or (Yellow)
Unsurpassable (Yellow)

Tulip
Bellona (Yellow)
Bing Crosby (Red)
Charles (Red)
Christmas Marvel (Pink)
Golden Eddy (Red, var.
    with yellow or cream)
Hibernia (White)
Karel Doorman (Red, var.
    with yellow or cream)
Kees Nelis (Red, var.
    with yellow or cream)
Olaf (Red)
Ornament (Yellow)
Paul Richter (Red)
Peerless Pink (Pink)
Preludium (Pink)
Prominence (Red)
Stockholm (Red)
Thule (Yellow with red)

A sheaf of wheat on the front
door makes an
attractive alternative to a
wreath. Tied with a
pretty ribbon,
it can be attached
with a nail.

Outdoor Decorations

I n addition to lights and
garlands, there are other
outdoor decorations with
which to embellish your
house and yard. Your creations don't
have to be elaborate but they can be
impressive with the use of materials
that are easy to obtain.

Well-proportioned trees or
substantial ornamental bushes may
make appropriate outdoor Christmas
trees when decorated with bows and
ornaments and threaded with garlands of miniature, outdoor lights.

Strings of cranberries are traditional garlands for trees inside.
They can also hang off trees outside
as food for the birds. Cranberries will
attract catbirds, grosbeaks, robins,
and starlings.

Sometimes a search through the
garage or garden shed will yield finds
suitable for outdoor decorations. For
example, wheelbarrows—especially
old wood ones—can become attractive displays. They don't even have
to be in working order. Dress them
up in Christmas finery, fill them with
boxes covered and tied with vinyl or
plastic wrapping, and park the wheel-
barrow on the front lawn. Cast-off
sleds and toboggans can be used in
the same way.

Instead of the usual evergreen
wreath on the front door, consider
an arrangement of dried grasses and
herbs tied with a large, red ribbon.

Vinyl or plastic ribbon, which is
weatherproof and available in many
colors, is a good material for wrapping pillars, posts, or a mailbox support. Hobby and variety stores carry
Styrofoam stars and candy canes that
can be decorated and used outdoors.

In many parts of the country,
there is very little color in the yard
during the winter. Pots of poinsettias
or other cold-weather plants can
contribute lively splashes of red to a
landscape that may look a bit barren.
Group several pots together on the
front porch or use individual pots
spaced at regular intervals to define
the edges of a path or a planting bed.

Topiary is usually associated with formal gardens, but at Christmastime it can be used advantageously to sculpt bushes, above, or trees, below, into shapes appropriate to the season. Some miniature lights are sufficient adornment for these living decorations.

117

Make sure that guests approaching your front door know that they are visiting a household that enjoys and celebrates Christmas. Light their way with candles flanking the path, opposite page. Show them you expect greeting cards by wrapping the mailbox, left. Or, pull out an old-fashioned sleigh and park it on the front lawn, below.

Christmas Cutouts

If you have the time and tools to make something a little special, you might want to construct some wood cutout figures. Decorations such as this modern version of Santa's sleigh or the depiction of Rudolph, seen on the next page, can be set up along a path or on the front lawn.

Wood cutout figures are not difficult to make. Decide on the shapes you want, then draw them on paper. Realize that gentle curves and angles are easier to cut than complex contours. Transfer the outlines to pieces of exterior-grade plywood and cut around them with a saber saw. Coat plywood shapes with sealer and, using exterior-grade paint, add details. Painting the shapes is a particularly suitable project for children.

A fence makes an especially dramatic stage set for the cutouts. They can be arranged along the entire length, and attached with appropriate hardware. For freestanding shapes, figures, or animals, use thicker plywood. Also, realize that winter winds may create a problem. Braces attached to the back side help prevent the figures from toppling over. Construct braces so that they lie flat on the ground, and weight them with bags filled with sand.

Encourage the whole family to participate in deciding what kinds of forms to construct. You can create an entire scene, with Santa Claus arriving on a sled pulled by reindeer, or a marching band of toy soldiers, or a crèche full of imaginary animals. At night, illuminate the figures with footlights to give the effect of actors on stage. Position the lights so that you get dramatic shadows on the fence background or

snowy ground. The cutouts can be stored and used year after year. New characters can be added each Christmas or the original ones can be repainted in order to set a different scene.

The same technique (cutting out and painting exterior-grade plywood) can be used to make letters that spell out holiday greetings to anyone passing by. Choose your message, cut out the necessary wood letters, paint them in bright colors, and arrange them outdoors.

Finding a suitable location for your cutouts should not be difficult. Christmas greetings and decorations can be attached to a fence in front of your house, suspended on

rope or sturdy monofilament from a tree branch, or attached to your house. Decorations can even be positioned on the roof as long as you devise a way to mount them that will hold them firmly in place without damaging the roofing materials.

If you live in an apartment, letters can be wired to the railing around a deck or balcony.

A walkway or driveway makes a particularly good site for outdoor decorations. Wooden cutouts or luminarias (see page 132) arranged along the edges will welcome and guide guests to the front door.

The Magic Of Light

Twinkling bulbs, dancing reflections, and the glow of candlelight all add to the magic of Christmas

Along with the scent of fresh fir branches or baking gingerbread, the spectacle of a decorated tree, and the taste of nutmeg-sprinkled eggnog, effective lighting evokes the magic of Christmas. The source of light, be it flame, ornamental bulbs, or glowing lamps, should enchant the eye. Enchantment lies more often in reflected light: the luster of a grouping of silver glass balls on a brightly lit table, the amber glow of candlelight skillfully augmented by concealed electric lights, or the crispness of a white Colonial facade illuminated by floodlights.

Light was a central element in the ancient observances of winter solstice, which led to bonfires, hearth fires, and burning candles becoming traditional parts of Christmas. The early symbolic meanings of fire later referred to Christ, the Light of the World. The ancient Hebrew festival known as Hanukkah was called the Feast of Lights. It occurs in the ninth month of the Jewish calendar, which corresponds to the Christmas season. Candles, lamps, and the traditional seven-branch candlestick were used to light the Temple.

Today, even the most secular celebration relies heavily on the use of light. After all, it wouldn't be Christmas without twinkling bulbs on the tree, a glow at the table, and a merry display on the lawn.

Light always adds a special magic. It can be the sparkling strands of outdoor lights decorating the trees and bushes, preceding pages, the soft glow of candles, left, or the blaze of an open fire, opposite page.

Setting the Stage

To prove that a decorated tree is like a spotlit actor, look how the room, top, is a bare stage compared to the same room, above.

The chief function of holiday lighting, indoors and out, is to create or enhance a fantasy, or at least a special mood. Think of holiday lighting as a stage effect that makes the home into a world apart from the outside. This transformation happens by bathing the environment in just the right glow and by highlighting some features while hiding or de-emphasizing others.

The difference between uninspiring and successful holiday lighting lies in understanding the basics of lighting and some quirks of human perceptual psychology. Give some thought to these matters before creating Christmas magic with lights.

Color

How we see color is determined by the light that makes it visible. We have built-in emotional reactions to color as we see it. Therefore, effective lighting, together with appropriate use of color, gives rooms moods that we can feel deeply.

In decorating for Christmas, creating an atmosphere of warmth and coziness is the basic objective. Selecting warm colors, in the red-orange-gold range of the spectrum, is important. But so is using light that reveals these colors in all their warmth. Daylight does. Firelight does, even more emphatically, by de-emphasizing cooler colors. Incandescent light from low-wattage bulbs underscores warm colors better than more intense incandescent light, which is far whiter. Low-voltage light is slightly less warm than light of the same intensity from 120-volt lamps, because composition of bulb filaments is different. To some extent you can control the warmth of spotlights and floodlights by using tinted bulbs or filters.

Colored lamps can easily distort color, rather than enhance it. Blue or bluish light, used outdoors, casts cool shadows and enhances the greenness of foliage. Green light emphasizes foliage, though a bit unnaturally. Used indoors, blue or green light gives the colors of skin, food, and many decorations and furnishings a blatant eeriness. Yellow and amber light makes outdoor foliage look pale and unhealthy; red light renders it brown and deathly.

Aside from distortion caused by some colored lights, another danger is overuse. Rather than enhancing colors and making for a pleasant atmosphere, lights of too many colors create a carnival atmosphere. Selecting a single, appropriate color can unify the surroundings and soothe the emotions. This doesn't mean, of course, that a Christmas tree with multicolored lights is ineffective. Widespread mixing of colored decorative lights or flood- and spotlights indoors or out creates disunity and garishness.

Light Sources

The position of a light source in relation to people in the lighted area can enhance their comfort. A poorly placed light can create discomfort, even distress.

A thoughtlessly placed light can make a blinding glare, which is annoying and uncomfortable in a sitting area, and dangerous around stairs, garden walkways, and rooms with furniture that is easy to trip over. Outdoors and indoors, position spot- and floodlights so they shine on decorations and displays but not into bystander's eyes. Bullet reflectors and other kinds of fixtures can help to focus light and eliminate glare outside the focal area.

Candles burning at eye level on a dining table obstruct diners' view across the table and inhibit conversation. On the other hand, a bank of table-level votive candles casts a golden glow over diners and dining table and contributes to the festive mood of a holiday celebration.

Lighting at a bathroom mirror can create effects grim enough to squelch any guest's holiday merriment. A light placed high and shining downward results in the appearance of a heavy chin, puffy eyes with dark circles, a prominent nose, and deep lines. In contrast, flanking the mirror with lights eliminates unflattering shadows and illuminates the face evenly, making for reassurance and good cheer.

Indoor Lighting

Inside, light, more than any other element, creates atmosphere: a pervasive feeling of hospitality and coziness, of sparkling festivity, or of sophisticated elegance. Each of these and other moods can predominate in different parts of your house and at different times.

Using directional lights to illuminate Christmas decorations such as a wreath on a wall or a fruit pyramid on a table underscores their seasonal beauty. Similarly, appropriate furnishings and attractive architectural details can be illuminated to emphasize their beauty. A lighted quilt displayed on a wall strikes a charming, old-fashioned note. Handsome beveled paneling above a mantel can be softly lighted to accentuate its detailing, by glowing candles on the mantel or by discreetly positioned electric lights.

Practicality

The main purpose of holiday lighting is to create atmosphere or evoke magic. A less dramatic but no less important purpose is purely practical: to make the celebration of Christmas easy and safe. Without breaking the spell desired, practical lighting makes hosts or guests more comfortable in or around the house.

During the Christmas season you will require additional illumination. For an afternoon party, for example, you might set up a serving table that calls for special lighting. Similarly, at a buffet dinner, otherwise adequate general illumination may be insufficient for serving and dining. Anticipating and meeting particular needs makes for a more enjoyable, relaxed holiday season.

Another type of practical lighting needed outside as well as inside the house is informational lighting. The function is to tell people where things are, for convenience or safety.

After you have hung all the Christmas decorations, move your lamps around to spotlight the effect you have created.

127

Fixtures

Nearly every kind of indoor fixture is potentially useful during Christmas, and there are many types and styles to choose from.

Whatever your lighting requirements, it's likely that with little effort and expense you can adapt existing fixtures to serve holiday needs. You may decide to buy portable fixtures for use all year, which can be adapted for Christmas. You may find that you should remove existing fixtures and substitute more serviceable ones. Standard recessed downlights, for instance, can be replaced by swiveling-eyeball downlights, which you can adjust to the needs of the season.

Clamp-on fixtures, which offer maximum flexibility, can accommodate reflector bulbs for flooding or spotting. Table, floor, wall, and hanging lamps, depending upon style and construction, may serve single or multiple functions. Those with translucent shades offer general illumination or can accent a particular corner of the room, depending on the strength of the bulb. Adjustable fixtures such as flexible arm (architects') lamps also permit lateral or angled lighting. Track lighting is extremely flexible. Individual canisters inserted in the tracks can be adjusted to send light in any direction.

Intensity

Accent decorations and other desirable features. Let the rest of the environment glow softly or melt into shadow. In creating atmosphere with light, understatement can be dramatic. If the overhead lights at a movie theater weren't dimmed, the audience could never lose themselves in even the most engrossing thriller.

On the other hand, light of a slightly higher intensity in one room or area, relative to the surrounding

light, can enable hosts to manage their guests deftly. Light intensity below the point of harshness draws people toward it. Making light in a living room about 20 percent brighter than that in an entry hall encourages guests to come directly into the living room. Once they're there, the brighter light enhances their feeling of well-being. If a dining room is about 20 percent dimmer than adjacent rooms it will discourage guests from entering before the host is ready for them.

Simplicity

A small room with a tree, a fruit pyramid, a bank of poinsettias, three wall wreaths, and a display of Christmas cards, all ablaze with light, confounds the eye. Although the space can accommodate several decorations and displays, the effect is pleasing when only one, or a unified grouping, is lighted for contemplation from any one vantage point.

Lighting has the capacity to dictate what is looked at and how it is seen. Make the most of its potential for enhancing the enjoyment of Christmas by keeping it, and the objects it illuminates, simple.

Above: Strands of lights can be taped around window frames for a sparkle that will also be seen outside. Opposite page: An elaborate candelabra cannot be moved, but it can be put on a dimmer switch or fitted with special bulbs for Christmas lighting effects.

In many parts of the country, neighbors get together to create spectacular effects. The lakeside homeowners, above, used the same technique of outlining the buildings in light as was used in the Plaza in Kansas City, opposite page.

Outdoor Lighting

When a yard is illuminated like an airport it lacks magic, even if the house and decorations are splendid. Harsh lighting washes out both color and mood.

Outdoor lighting sets the holiday tone, either buoyant or serene, for family, guests, and passersby. A lighted tableau makes a dramatic seasonal statement: Santa with his sleigh and reindeer transforms a roof or a front yard into a realm of light-hearted fantasy; a Nativity scene depicts the Genesis, and very essence, of the Christmas celebration. Blue shadows can be cast across the snowy contours of a lawn with a floodlight and a daylight-blue filter. The glow, as soft as moonlight, will intensify the pristine beauty of the winter night and enhance the setting of the house. Trees or shrubs, strung with lights to proclaim the holiday, hint at the festive spirit that exists indoors. A floodlit house embellished with

holiday greenery, together with a spotlit tree of unusual beauty, pleases all who see it and welcomes visitors.

Safety
Using light to define the outdoors, particularly if the route from street or parking area is dark, is a matter of safety and comfort. Marking the entry to the driveway by illuminating the shrubbery that flanks it serves to orient and invite visitors. It also lends visual depth to a lighted outdoor display. Bends, uneven surfaces, and steps in a walkway should be illuminated throughout the year to prevent false steps.

During the holidays, particularly when outdoor decorations tend to distract visitors, this kind of informational lighting becomes imperative. Aside from using permanent post lights, garden lamps, carefully positioned spotlights, and low path lights, you might consider defining the path to the door more festively.

For special occasions, consider flanking a path Mexican-style with rows of paper bags, each ballasted with sand and holding a lighted candle. If the landscaping includes shrubs on either side of a walkway, string them with clear miniature lights. This defines the path and at the same time gives visitors a holiday welcome.

Tree Lights
In the late 1950s, Chicago lighting expert George Silvestri and Joe Kreis, display director of Saks Fifth Avenue, collaborated on a lighting display that was to help revolutionize home and public Christmas lighting. They decorated the bare elms along the sidewalks in front of Saks with strings of tiny clear lights that Silvestri had imported from Italy. Today the entire length of the Magnificent Mile on Michigan

Luminarias

At Christmastime in towns and cities throughout the Southwest, small lanterns illuminate walkways, buildings, and plazas with twinkling lights. Luminarias originated in Spain and Old Mexico and were adopted in the western states during the seventeenth and eighteenth centuries.

Nowadays, most luminarias are made from simple brown paper bags. You can use supermarket shopping bags but these are likely to be creased, wrinkled, and printed with the name of the store. Depending on the number of lights you need, you may want to purchase new bags that are packed flat. Choose only one size or buy various-sized bags to create an arrangement of contrasting heights. You'll also need small, fat, white or colored votive candles; glass jars, candle holders, or dishes to support the candles; and sand or fine gravel to weight the bags.

Assembly is very simple. Open a paper bag, and fold down the top two or three times to form a cuff. Pour in sand to give the bag weight and stability. Prepare as many bags as needed, then arrange them in the selected sites. Lastly, set a holder and lit candle in each luminaria.

Early luminarias were sometimes made of colorfully patterned papers imported from the Orient. You can purchase or make bags in any color or pattern. Another idea is to punch holes in the bags or cut out designs to add extra sparkle. Don't cut away too much, however, or the effect will be ruined and the bag will be weakened.

Never leave burning candles unattended either outside of or inside the house and keep children away from the flames. As pretty as these decorations are, they can be dangerous.

Avenue is decorated with miniature lights during Christmas. The popularity of outdoor lights has skyrocketed around the country and throughout the world.

In selecting Christmas lights, consider your needs as well as the specifications of the various types and brands of lights. Read the general information about Christmas tree lights on page 136. Compare features and quality of the brands available to you. Be certain that you choose a type and brand certified safe for outdoor use.

When decorating an outdoor Christmas tree, particularly a large tree with C9-lights (see page 137), it's easy to simplify the process and at the same time protect living branches from clips and hot bulbs. Instead of attaching lights directly to the tree, attach them with floral tape to guide wires that extend from near the top of the tree to pegs or hooks in the ground along the circumference of the outermost bottom foliage, or just outside this circle. As an alternative, attach light strands more directly, using ornament hooks.

Fixtures

Well lights, especially suited for uplighting outdoor Christmas trees, shrubs, and walls, are available in standard- and low-voltage models. Well lights are sunk into the ground. Maybe you will use these permanent fixtures only at Christmas, or you may decide to use them in the garden throughout the year.

Bullet lights shield bulbs from the elements and cut glare. These cone-shaped fixtures may be permanently or temporarily attached. Some bullet lights have plastic or glass lenses, which safeguard against damage to bulbs from moisture or sudden temperature changes.

A pair of well-manicured trees acts as guards on either side of a decorated house. Their Christmas uniform is strands of lights wound around their girths.

Garlands of lights cloak a deciduous tree denuded by an eastern winter.

133

A Victorian house—
decorative enough the year
around—gets an
added fillip with the addition
of miniature lights.

Other outdoor lights for spotting or flooding may be unprotected fixtures. Attached temporarily or permanently to the house, outlying structures, or trees, they may be portable and have spikes for positioning in the ground.

Bulbs
The most commonly used bulb for outdoor spotlighting and floodlighting is a parabolic aluminized reflector (PAR) lamp. Low-voltage PARs and other reflector bulbs are readily available. Quartz incandescent bulbs, which operate at a higher temperature and give brighter light than ordinary incandescent lights, can be found in both regular- and low-voltage versions.

For lighting very large outdoor areas brightly, mercury vapor, high-

pressure sodium, and metal halide lamps are available, though not commonly used for residential lighting.

You might consider using filters in conjunction with reflector lights to create special effects indoors or out: for example, a daylight-blue filter or a dichroic filter (available from display shops) produces light with three-colored shadows.

Displays
Along with the family Christmas tree, a lighted outdoor display probably gives more pleasure to children than any other Christmas decoration. Tastefully designed and well

lighted, it delights adults, too. The outdoor positioning allows the whole community to enjoy it.

A key to effectiveness is simplicity. Create only one scene or central feature. This might be Santa and his reindeer, the Nativity, or a group of carolers. You can enhance the scene, however, by incorporating the house, or part of it, and maybe a tree that is either spotted or silhouetted. One or more daylight-blue flood-lights concealed in a tree on a snowy lawn create dappled blue shadows from the branches and a moonlit context for the lighted scene. Be careful to avoid making a disunified display with too many, or unrelated, elements.

Flat figures can be lighted with only one floodlight. In creating a scene with three-dimensional figures, however, light it with at least two PAR bulbs from different angles. Lighting with more than one spot makes for even illumination and eliminates harsh shadows. Both lights can be floods, or one can be a spot that emphasizes focal features. Conceal lights on or close to the ground, at a distance more or less that of the largest dimension of the display. Remember that colored light distorts some other colors, that poor positioning of lights creates glare, and that overly intense lighting washes out color and destroys mood.

These homeowners have gone all out in their outdoor lighting efforts. The trees, the shrubs, the windows, and a large star-shaped wreath proclaim that it is Christmas for this family.

A second home—even if it is a boat—also deserves to be decorated.

Lighting The Christmas Tree

Originally, trees were lit with candles—but it is not recommended that you continue this dangerous tradition. Nowadays there are many safe and attractive alternatives. Lights for the Christmas tree come in many shapes, sizes, and colors.

Types of Tree Lights

Most strands of lights sold today incorporate technical advances over the old-fashioned types that darken entirely when one bulb burns out, necessitating frustrating, potentially destructive rummaging through the lights and delicate ornaments of a fully decorated tree in order to test each light. Although a burned-out bulb doesn't extinguish a whole strand of modern lights, a damaged bulb with a broken filament will darken an entire strand of some brands of miniature lights. Know what you're buying.

Do you want strings with straight line or loop construction? You'll most likely want straight-line strands,

because loops are difficult to use, and even coverage is hard to achieve. Loop lights are becoming less popular, and many tree lights sold at bargain prices are loop sets being closed out of an inventory. If you want straight-line construction, do you want single-end strings with piggy-back connections, or end-to-end (add-on) strings?

Do you want transparent, translucent, or pearlized lights (translucent lights with a glow that has a pearlescent quality)? Do you want clear ("white"), single-colored, or multi-colored lights?

As you compare prices, take into account the number of lights per string, spacing, overall length, and length of the lead wire (between plug and fuse light), especially of strands with piggyback plugs. Try to determine how well constructed a set is.

You'll also want to decide whether to purchase one or more of the fancier styles of lights. Some of the options are novelty, bubble, flasher, twinkle, and chaser lights. There are scores of novelty lights, with bulbs that are covered with or surrounded by such translucent or reflective ornaments as globes, angels, ice crystals

or icicles, candles, doves, drums, lanterns, stars, and pinecones. Strands of novelty lights are often used on a tree in addition to strands of basic lights. Most bubble lights purchased today are miniature lights. Lighted treetop decorations—angels, stars, and other images—are widely sold. An entire set of flasher lights blinks on and off; a flasher plug can make any string of lights flash. Twinkle lights blink individually, at random. Often they are interspersed with steadily burning lights on the same strand. Lights of a chaser strand blink in sequence.

Always be mindful of safety. Check to determine whether a brand bears the UL seal, which means that it has been tested and approved by Underwriters Laboratories. (Other organizations endorse brands meeting their safety standards.) Does each strand have a fuse, and, if so, is it easily replaceable with a readily obtainable fuse? Do the printed directions clearly indicate how many strings may be safely connected to each other or to a common plug, or do they at least indicate total wattage of each string? How hot do bulbs get?

Miniature Lights

Bulbs push rather than screw into place. Special strings of extrabright bulbs are offered by some companies. Bulbs from one strand of lights often aren't interchangeable with those of another strand because of differences in voltage. On artificial and living trees, use the coolest of Christmas tree lights (miniatures are cool enough, when properly attached). They are far more energy efficient than other lights, and small enough to look attractive in wreaths and on other Christmas decorations for which other lights would be too large or hot. The clear lights are particularly popular and versatile.

C6-lights: These are less common now than any other tree lights. Most C6-lights sold are replacement bulbs

Lighting options are well displayed in many home centers and hardware stores across the country.

for old strands. Bulbs screw into their sockets.

C7-lights: These are what first come to mind when we think of indoor Christmas lights. Some brands are certified safe for outdoor decoration. Bulbs screw into their sockets. The cool-burning bulbs are usually five rather than seven watts. Nevertheless, they are fairly warm and therefore liable to damage artificial or living trees, unlike miniature, and they dry cut trees faster than miniature lights.

C9-lights: Larger than C7s, and with larger screw-in bases, C9s (a seldom used designation) are made for outdoor use. Cool-burning C9s are usually seven rather than nine watts. Even these bulbs can damage living trees and shrubs, unless they are carefully positioned and attached so lamps don't touch foliage or branches. Their use as decorations for windows, eaves, and other architectural and landscape features has declined in favor of subtler, cooler-burning and more energy-efficient miniature lights.

Lighting a Dense Tree
If a tree is dense and solid, the lights should be placed on the surface. Always work downward from the top of the tree. String lights in a random pattern, in vertical strings, horizontal rows, scalloped tiers, or a single spiral or parallel spirals originating at the top. End-to-end lights lend themselves better than single-end lights to these formations. Avoid jarring bulbs against each other or against floor or walls; the delicate filaments are easily broken, and bulbs and socket wires are easily dislodged.

One formula for estimating the number of lights needed for solid coverage of a dense tree is to multiply the height of the tree by the diameter at the widest point, then multiply the answer by three. For less solid coverage, decorating in a pattern, or accenting the shape, multiply height times largest diameter times two.

Lighting an Open Tree
If a tree is open branched, it will need lighting throughout, not just on the surface. Following the procedure outlined here, instead of randomly scattering lights, will produce even coverage and a pleasing effect. Every branch will be distinct.

As with a solid tree, start at the top and work downward. Above eye level, run cords along tops of branches; below eye level, conceal cords beneath branches. Be sure that lights always point upward and sit above foliage. Work from the trunk outward to the end of each branch, then along the other side of the branch back to the trunk. Next, moving consistently either clockwise or counterclockwise, wire adjacent branch at that level. When you have gone around the tree, decorating every branch at that level, drop to the next level of branches and continue to use the out-and-back pattern of coverage. This pattern results in attractive, even distribution of lights and prevents tangles caused by crossed wires.

Prevent strands from getting tangled by wrapping them into a bracelet.

Amount of Lights Needed
For a generously lighted, open-branched tree, a rule of thumb for determining how many lights are needed is two 35-light strings per foot of tree height. For a tree with an especially wide base, such as a typical noble fir, use three strings of 35 lights per foot.

If a single extension cord is insufficient, attach one midway up the tree and another near the base. You'll be using either end-to-end strands or single-end strands with piggyback (add-on) plugs. Never exceed manufacturer's recommendations for the number of strands that may be safely plugged together. Always connect piggyback plugs so that the plug of the uppermost strand is on top and plugs of successively lower strands are correspondingly closer to the electrical source.

Attaching Lights
Unless you're using bulbs that get hot enough to burn your hands, work with lighted strands so you can accurately judge where lights should be positioned. An extension cord fastened to a large tree about midway up the trunk brings the power source within reach of any single-end

Above: Start at the top of a tree and work your way down. Where neatness matters, fasten lights to branches with floral wire. Opposite page: The effect of a well-lit, decorated tree is one that will be remembered until next December.

attaching a false tip (either a stick or bamboo rod) to the top of the tree and fastening the ornament to the false tip.

Storing Light Strings

Remember that bulbs and, to a lesser extent, wires and sockets, are fragile. Although it's a time-consuming process, unscrew each bulb and store it insulated from other bulbs or hard surfaces. Because it's inconvenient to remove each miniature light bulb, you can protect them, and keep strings from tangling, by carefully winding strands around empty paper-towel rolls or 2-inch-wide strips of cardboard. Be sure that bulbs don't touch each other in storage, and strands are kept away from moisture and heat.

When you take light strings out of storage, be certain that the wires haven't cracked, thereby creating a safety hazard. Be sure each bulb is screwed or pushed into its socket, and wires connected to each socket are securely in place.

strand on the upper part of the tree. Whether you're working with end-to-end or single-end lights, the procedure is basically the same.

A professional tree decorator offers a tip for attaching lights to a tree. Although some strands have a clip at every light, instead use 22-gauge floral wire to fasten lights onto branches. Attach each light with only a half (180-degree) twist. Later, when removing lights, you'll be glad that the wires allow you to release the cord with a slight tug at every point of attachment. Not only does this method save time and effort, but it protects the branches of living trees from damage that clips might inflict.

Topping the Tree

Do you want a star, an angel, or another kind of lighted ornament at the treetop? Before setting it in place, be sure the tip is strong enough to support the weight. If you're lighting a living tree, protect the growing tip by

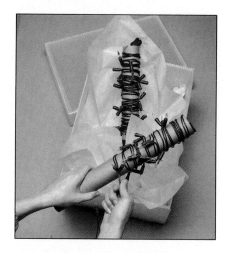

Use empty paper-towel rolls to store lights safely until next year. Cut slits in the cardboard at the top and the bottom to keep the strands from unwinding.

Candlelight

The burning and lighting of candles plays an important role in many ancient ceremonies. One of the most charming customs is the Swedish celebration of Santa Lucia.

Lucia was a beautiful, Roman maiden who refused to renounce her Christianity and was burned at the stake. Because her Saint's Day falls on December 13—the time of the year when days start to lengthen—it is an occasion to light candles.

In Swedish homes, the youngest daughter is usually chosen to be the Lucia Queen. Dressed in a white gown and crowned with lighted candles, she brings breakfast and a Christmas song to the members of her family.

Lit or unlit, candles bestow or at least suggest the warmth and reassurance that fire provides in the middle of winter. Some are scented, and the aroma—perhaps bayberry or pine or clove—adds a welcome dimension to the sensuous enjoyment of Christmas in the home.

As with all other uses of fire, particularly around drying evergreens, be mindful of the hazardous aspect of these lovely decorations. Place candles away from flammable materials, fasten them firmly in place, and burn them only when responsible adults are present.

Following are directions for making three different types of candles that you can use to decorate your home or give to friends during Christmas. Children love to make, or assist in making, candles, and for the most part the procedures here are simple and easy.

Some books recommend gathering materials at hand, such as string, crayons, and kitchen paraffin. You are safer, and your creations more predictable and dependable, if you use candle paraffin, stearic acid (an additive that makes paraffin tough, dense, and even burning), wicks, scents, and coloring manufactured specifically for candle-making and sold by craft shops. Otherwise,

Above: Crowning the youngest daughter with candles is how the Swedes celebrate Santa Lucia day.
Right: A heart-shaped chocolate mold acts as a candle holder for a Christmas display.

candles may burn dangerously hot and annoyingly smoky, or very poorly, and their smell may be noxious and unpleasant. Even with proper materials, there is a danger of overheating the wax to the point of combustion. To guard against this danger, use a double boiler, and always exercise caution. Hot wax can inflict serious, painful burns. Work in a well-ventilated place. Do not use water, except in the bottom of the double boiler.

Basic Large Candle

This substantial cylindrical candle is easy to make and burns for a long time. You can determine the color, add a scent, and incorporate the candle in many types of decorations. If children participate in the project they should be carefully supervised.

Paper frozen orange-juice cans (12 oz or larger), 1 can for each candle
Double boiler
Candle paraffin with a melting point of 125° F to 135° F
Stearic acid (triple-pressed is purest)
Cooking thermometer
Metal cooking ladle
Metal pitcher with handle
Old wooden spoon or stirrer
Liquid candle coloring
Ice cream sticks or pencils, 1 for each candle
15-ply candle wicking, "cooked" in wax
Metal washer, or wick holder from a craft shop, 1 for each candle
Oil-based candle scent (optional)
Small paring knife
Old nylon stocking

1. Prepare orange-juice cans making sure they are clean and dry.
2. In a double boiler melt candle paraffin, then add stearic acid (10 parts wax to 1 part acid, by weight). Let mixture heat no higher than 200° F. Carefully ladle hot mixture into pitcher. Add and stir in coloring.
3. Over each can lay and center an ice-cream stick with candle wicking

Above: Use storebought candles or make your own in a variety of shapes and sizes and group them together for a lavish display.
Left: If you run out of candlesticks, use apples as holders for candles on the dining table.

141

tied to it. Candle wicking should be weighted with washer at the end and long enough to touch bottom of can.
4. Fill can nearly full of hot wax mixture. Pour as close to center of can as possible to avoid bubbles. Add oil-based scent (if used) to each can.

When candle has hardened—at least 1 hour at 70° F room temperature, sometimes longer—cut wick flush with candle. Carefully tear away paper spiral that forms sides of the can. Turn candle so that the bottom becomes the top. Remove weight from wick and use a paring knife as necessary to shape top. Trim wick to about ½ inch in length.

If candle needs polishing, rub with the nylon stocking.

Flowerpot Candle

An ordinary terra-cotta flowerpot makes an excellent permanent container for a candle. Any pot up to 6 or 8 inches in diameter is suitable. If you are using pots 3 inches or less in diameter, use 15-ply wicking; for 4-inch pots, use 24-ply wicking; for larger pots use 30-ply wicking.

The Flowerpot Candle is made in the same way as the Basic Large Candle (see page 141), except that this candle remains permanently in its mold.

Use the same procedure and materials as for Basic Large Candle, minus orange-juice cans, plus:

Terra-cotta pots
Tape
Grout
Terra-cotta saucers (optional)
Mineral oil
Paper towels

Two days or so before you make candles, cover drainage holes in pots from the bottom with tape, and seal them from inside with grout. Rub surfaces of pots and tops and sides of saucers with mineral oil. Apply a second coat. After two hours rub surfaces dry with paper towels. This is to minimize or prevent uneven darkening of terra-cotta when it is permeated by molten wax. Continue with step 2 of Basic Large Candle.

Sand-Cast Candle

This attractively crude, somewhat irregular candle, with its grainy texture, is constructed by an ancient casting process. Perhaps even more than the two candles already described, making this one is particularly exciting for children, because there is even more opportunity for their creative participation and experimentation.

Use the same materials as for the Basic Large Candle (see page 141), minus the orange-juice cans, plus:

Fine screen
Clean sand
Pail, tub, or large pot
Wire or cotton wicking, (15-ply for 3-inch-dia candle, 24-ply for 4 inch dia, 30-ply for over 4 inch dia)

1. Strain sand through a screen to eliminate leaves, seaweed, and other organic matter or trash.
2. Pour sand into pail, moisten it slightly, and blend it until moisture is evenly distributed.
3. Scoop out sand or press into it to create a form for casting. You may want to shape tripod legs or a flat base for the candle. Usually natural rather than geometric forms are more appealing in sand-cast candles. Fine sand allows for finer details and textures than does coarse sand.

The dryer the sand and the hotter the wax, the thicker the sand crust on the candle will be, and the less chance you have to reproduce detailed patterns and textures that you have made in the sand.

Interesting layered effects may be achieved by casting the candles on a beach, where the natural layering of the sand hasn't been destroyed.
4. Attach wire wicking to a metal washer or wick holder. Set wick in place before pouring the wax. (Wire wick is rigid enough to stand upright if attached to a secure base.)

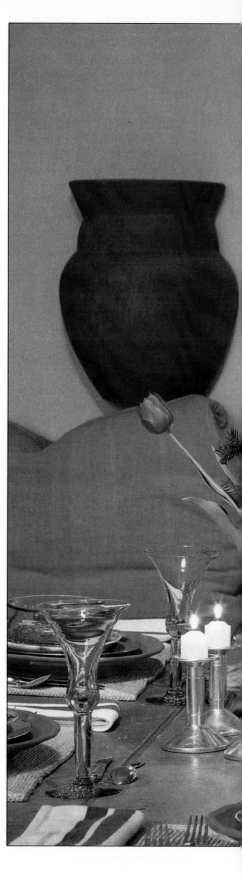

At a candlelit dinner be as
lavish with the light
as you are with the food
and the flowers.

CHAPTER 6

The Treats Of Christmas

Presenting food as a feast for the eye and a gift from the cook

Along with the decorated tree, food is probably the item most associated with the holiday season. Reminiscing about Christmases past usually conjures up memories of the aromas of baking bread, the anticipation of Christmas dinner, baskets full of nuts and fruit, chestnuts roasting on the fire, and special foods and drinks to be savored while wrapping presents, decorating the tree, addressing cards, or mulling over gift lists. To overlook food when discussing Christmas is like going to the beach without a picnic.

It is assumed that in your cookbook library you already have traditional and favorite recipes for whatever dishes you like to serve, that you can manage getting everything to the table hot, and that you have mastered the art of carving under scrutiny. It is also taken for granted that you know your family's taste preferences for the kinds of vegetables or desserts that are served. Only you know whether the much-maligned fruitcake is welcomed for dessert or used as a doorstop.

This chapter offers ideas for presenting food—on the table or as a gift—in a way that does justice to the effort involved in preparing it.

To keep up their energy, Christmas cooks can grab snacks from a basket of nuts, left, while preparing a box of gift-wrapped cookies, preceding pages, or trays of beautifully garnished hors d'oeuvres, opposite page.

Red Raspberry Vinegar

Tutti Frutti For Rudy

For Marc love Sara

Premiere October 1981

Contents Herb Vinegar

Fruit Syrup For Josie!

Cauliflower

Coarse Ground '82 Mustard

Green Peppercorn Mustard

From My Kitchen To Yours

Christmas is one time of year when you feel embarrassed to pay a visit or go to a party empty-handed. However well organized you think you are, there is always the last-minute invitation—usually from friends who were not on your gift list—to drop around for a drink. One solution is to buy and wrap small tokens and fill in the gift tags when they are needed. The other—usually far more welcome—solution is an offering from your kitchen. Forget the garish ties, the inappropriate knickknacks, the novelty items that merit one guffaw and then get thrown away. A homemade cake or jar of canned preserves beautifully presented is a gift you can be sure will be enjoyed.

In the summer, when fruits and vegetables are in abundance, go to work and prepare jellies, jams, and preserves; make chutneys and sauces. In the fall, bake fruitcakes so that they can age in time for Christmas, add herbs to bottles of vinegar, and pickled beets and onions.

Pickled Delicacies

Almost any food may be pickled. Vegetable pickles, including the all-time favorite cucumber, are either fresh-packed by a quick brining process or fermented for longer periods. Fruit pickles are made from fresh fruit simmered in a spicy sweet-sour syrup. Pickled meats or seafood are usually simply marinated for short periods and then refrigerated. Relishes are piquant blends of chopped or ground vegetables and fruits, spices, and vinegar. Chutneys are a type of relish prepared from chopped fruits, nuts, and spices.

The basic ingredient in pickling is vinegar. Distilled white vinegar gives pickles a sharp, tart taste; cider

Packed in a pretty bottle, jar, or basket, food makes a thoughtful gift.

vinegar lends a more mellow, fruity flavor. Malt or wine vinegars may also be used, although they will add a distinctive color and flavor to pickles.

Sugar balances the tartness of vinegar. White sugar is most commonly used, but brown sugar is sometimes called for in relishes and chutneys. If you wish, you can substitute honey for up to half the amount of sugar called for.

Salt is both a preservative and a flavoring. Pickling salt is available at most supermarkets, but if you can't find it, pure granulated salt is the next choice. Iodized and plain table salt are undesirable because they contain additives that may cloud brine and discolor pickles.

Following are a few canning recipes suitable to make for gifts.

Fruit Preserves

Jellies, jams, and other fruit preserves are easy to make. In a few short hours you can turn just-picked fruit into blue-ribbon specialties. Many types of fruit preserves can be made simply by cooking fruit with sugar.

Jellies are made from fruit juices boiled with sugar until they gel. Fine jellies are clear and shimmering. When cut they hold their shape. Soft jellies simmered with slivers of citrus peel fall into the category of marmalades. Jams are made from crushed or chopped fruit cooked until thick.

Conserves are a marriage of two or more fruits and often contain nuts and raisins. Butters are fruit purées reduced to spreadable consistency.

Flavored Vinegars

Presented in an attractive bottle, herb-flavored vinegar is a welcomed and useful gift that is simple to make.

For every quart of vinegar, you need about 4 ounces of fresh herbs or 2 ounces of dried ones. Use the herb of your choice; tarragon is a favorite. Wash fresh herbs, pat dry, and place a few sprigs in each sterilized bottle. Pour vinegar into hot sterilized bottles and cap tightly. Allow herbs to steep in vinegar for 5 to 6 weeks before using.

Pickled Onions

It is not difficult to find tiny pickling onions at this time of year.

5 quarts tiny white onions
1¼ cups salt
2½ quarts distilled white vinegar
2½ cups sugar
4 tablespoons mustard seed
3 tablespoons whole black peppercorns
4 tablespoons grated horseradish
1 small red pepper per pint
1 bay leaf per pint

1. Cover onions with boiling water. Let stand 2 minutes. Drain and cover with cold water. Peel.
2. Sprinkle onions with salt and cover with water. Let stand overnight.
3. Drain onions. Rinse well with cold water and drain again.
4. Combine vinegar, sugar, mustard seed, peppercorns, and horseradish in large pot. Boil 2 minutes.
5. Add onions; bring to boil again.
6. Pack onions into clean, hot jars. Add pepper and bay leaf to each jar. Fill with boiling syrup, leaving ½-inch headspace; seal.
7. Process in boiling-water bath 10 minutes.
Yields 7 to 8 pints.

Marinara Sauce

Turn vine-ripened tomatoes into this well-seasoned tomato sauce.

3 tablespoons olive oil
1 large onion, chopped
2 cloves garlic, minced
4 pounds very ripe tomatoes,
   peeled, seeded, and puréed
2 teaspoons finely chopped
   fresh oregano
   or 1 teaspoon dried oregano
2 teaspoons finely chopped
   fresh basil
   or 1 teaspoon dried basil
Pinch of sugar
Salt and pepper, to taste

1. Heat oil in heavy skillet. Sauté onion until limp and transparent. Add garlic and sauté 30 seconds.
2. Stir in tomato purée and seasonings. Cook over medium-high heat, stirring frequently, until liquid is reduced and sauce thickens. Adjust seasonings to taste.
Yields about 2 pints.

To Freeze Cool sauce to room temperature. Spoon into rigid freezer containers. (Sauce swells when it freezes. Leave ½-inch headspace in a pint container.)

Gingered Peach Pickles

These peaches look good in a jar and they are delicious over ice cream.

8 pounds (about 3½ quarts)
   small peaches
3 pounds light brown sugar
1 quart cider vinegar
1-inch piece ginger root, peeled
   and crushed
2 tablespoons whole cloves,
   crushed
3 cinnamon sticks, broken up
1 whole clove per peach
1 cinnamon stick per quart
1 tablespoon brandy per
   quart (optional)

1. Peel peaches. Halve and pit or leave whole.
2. To prevent darkening, dip peaches into solution of 2 tablespoons vinegar, 2 tablespoons salt, and 1 gallon water. Rinse.
3. Combine sugar and vinegar in a large pot; bring to a boil over medium heat and boil 5 minutes. Tie ginger root, crushed cloves, and broken cinnamon sticks loosely in cheesecloth. Add to syrup and simmer 5 minutes.

4. Stick a whole clove in each peach half. Add only enough peaches to the simmering syrup to fill one of the quart jars; cook until peaches are hot but not soft (about 2 minutes). Do not overcook. Remove peaches with slotted spoon and pack tightly in clean, hot jar with a small stick of cinnamon. Repeat process until all peaches are packed in jars.
5. Bring syrup to a boil; remove spice bag. Pour hot syrup over peaches in jars, leaving ½-inch headspace. Add 1 tablespoon brandy to each jar, if desired. Seal.
6. Process in boiling-water bath for 15 minutes.
Yields 3 to 4 quarts.

Raisinberry Relish

This zestful, colorful relish makes a fine accompaniment for ham, game, or the holiday bird.

2¼ cups golden raisins
2 cups orange juice
1 cup water
¼ cup lemon juice
⅔ cup sugar
3 cups fresh or frozen cranberries
1 tablespoon finely grated
   orange peel

1. In a 3-quart saucepan, combine raisins, orange juice, the water, lemon juice, and sugar. Bring to a boil, stirring to dissolve sugar. Reduce heat. Simmer 10 minutes.
2. Add cranberries and simmer 5 minutes. Add orange peel and simmer about 5 minutes more, until liquid barely covers solid ingredients. Cool. Store, covered, in refrigerator up to 1 month.
Yields about 4½ cups.

To Freeze Spoon relish into labeled containers and freeze up to 1 year.

Using these recipes, make jars of Marinara Sauce, above, Gingered Peach Pickles, left, and Raisinberry Relish, opposite page.

Set a Sumptuous Table

T he tree is bought and trimmed; the living room is decorated; the wreath is hung on the front door; guests have been invited; and the menu is carefully planned to include favorite holiday dishes. Now make sure that when the doorbell rings the table will reflect all the hard work that went on in the kitchen.

Many traditional table decorations are still the most attractive centerpieces: elegant candle holders with tapers in various colors; flowers and potted plants, either purchased or from your garden; and pinecones, candy canes, winter fruit, and other seasonal items.

Simple or sumptuous, a Christmas decoration in the center of the dining or serving table provides a focus of beauty that can be enjoyed from many vantage points. The centerpiece can be as simple as a vase of flowers, a pot of forced bulbs, or a crystal bowl filled with Christmas ornaments. For something a little bit more special, make an arrangement in a bowl, basket, or tray.

Make sure your compositions match or complement the other accessories and the table linen, which might be a runner made out of red and green fabric. Tie napkins with ribbon bows that match bows in the centerpiece. Wire miniature pinecones or sprigs of flowers to napkin holders or to stems of wine glasses. Tape place cards to toothpicks or floral picks and stick them into pieces of fruit or pinecones. Light each place setting with a votive candle set in a small glass holder.

In England, crackers are traditional decorations at Christmas parties. These are cylinders wrapped in crepe paper. When pulled, a strip of paper inside breaks with a bang and the contents—usually paper

hats, party favors, and fortunes—spill out onto the table. Although they are carried by some specialty stores, crackers are hard to find. However, it would not be difficult to make your own version. Or, simply wrap some amusing surprises in each napkin.

Tall, Conical Arrangement

To suggest a Christmas tree, cover a cone-shaped piece of plastic foam with Spanish moss and decorate it with evergreen foliage and an array of fruits, vegetables, pods, and berries. This decoration is inappropriate on a dining table because of the height, but it would make a striking adornment on a buffet or serving table.

Long, Low Arrangement

On a dining table, a long, low arrangement is a suitable shape. To make the base, cut loaves of floral foam into pieces that will form the desired shape and size. Arrange the

Napkins can be folded in numerous ways: Arrange them in stem glasses, opposite page, or make bows by fanning out the ends after slipping on a napkin ring.

pieces and wrap them together in chicken wire. If the arrangement will contain fresh flowers, saturate the wired form with water and attach it to a tray or platter with floral clay; then add water to the tray.

Make fresh cuts on all living stems and decorate the form as desired, adding touches such as sprigs of mistletoe and holly in keeping with the Christmas spirit.

The food, the guests, the setting, and the centerpiece are all responsible for bringing the Christmas spirit to the table. To spare yourself last-minute work, here are some centerpieces that can be made beforehand, displayed on side tables, then placed on the dining table when you set it. For a quiet dinner at home, left, tuck apples, sprigs of berries, and pinecones into a basket full of traditional greenery. Even without the evergreen branches, apples, below, make a delicious decoration. Keep extras on hand to replenish the centerpiece after it has been raided by elves. Poinsettia plants, opposite page, can come to the table, pots and all. But they are more attractive if the pots are somewhat obscured. The containers can be wrapped in tissue or, as seen here, ringed with wreaths of twined branches.

The only danger of decorating with fruit is that it may be eaten before or during the time it is on display. These arrangements should be marked "hands off until after Christmas" or composed of artificial fruit. A pineapple (the Colonial American symbol of hospitality) is displayed, right, with a background of fanned leaves and a pedestal of apples and lemons. The fruit cone, opposite page top, drips with fruit not readily available in the winter. Eliminate the temptation to taste by using papier mâché, glass, raffia, or plastic imitations of fruit. Pomegranates and grapes, opposite page below, make a delicious-looking centerpiece that can be served as dessert after Christmas dinner.

Above: Thick slices of cucumber form cups that are filled with herbed cheese and topped with salmon, dill, and a caper. Below: An orange half contains an individual serving of cranberry sauce.

Decorating With Taste

To welcome your guests you've covered the tree in ornaments, swagged the mantel with evergreens, hung a wreath on the door, arranged the flowers, and polished the silver. Now what about the food you are going to serve? Doesn't that deserve to be decorated, too? Clever garnishes can make a trayful of even cheese and crackers appear special.

The only difficulty with serving food that both looks and tastes delicious is the amount of preparation time required. With a little practice, some dexterity, and a selection of icing tips, you can decorate cakes and pastries with graceful swirls and elegant ornaments. And, given some vegetables and a sharp knife, radish roses and mushroom rosettes can roll off your chopping board.

Garnishes

The photographs on these pages show food prepared by professional stylists to look appealing—that is the main purpose of a garnish. But don't overlook the fact that decorating food can be a way to add spice as well as visual appeal. Garnishes don't have to be complicated. Scooped-out potatoes topped with a cloud of sour cream and sprinkled with just a little caviar are easy to prepare and will delight guests.

Be daring and inventive with garnishes; they don't have to be eaten. If your guests do not care for kiwifruit with their trout, they can push it to one side. But when the trout appears on the table adorned with rings of this delicate green fruit and topped with red tomato roses it looks so much more interesting than a fish covered in white sauce.

Another reason for garnishing is to add zest and texture to a dish. Spears of endive radiating around a circle of stuffed potatoes are crunchy accompaniments to the soft crab filling. Individual containers made out of orange halves add a surprising citrus tang to the cranberry sauce inside. Sprays and sprigs of almond-paste flowers and leaves add a nutty taste that cuts the sweetness of chocolate frosting.

Garnishes add color, an important point to remember when serving an otherwise monocolor meal such as poached fish with rice and cauliflower—especially if it is served on a white plate. The color of the garnish can be coordinated with your table setting, or you can make all your dishes red and green in honor of the season.

However tasty the food you serve, it will be that much better if the presentation is appetizing.

Molds and Shapes

Another way to make food particularly appealing is to present it in eye-catching molded or cut shapes.

Cake, cookie, and tart tins come in a large variety of shapes and sizes. Some have removable bases so that a baked cake or pie, resplendent with fluted edges, can easily be lifted out. Others come in interesting shapes such as a *Kugelhopf* mold in which you bake a cake ring, then fill the center with ingredients of your choice. Specialty pans such as madeleine molds and brioche pans are available in kitchen-supply stores. Then, of course, there are cookie cutters. Although they are generally used to cut dough, they can also be used to shape cold cuts or individual servings of pâté or cheese.

Crystallized Flowers

Lovely edible decorations, crystallized flowers also make elegant desserts. Choose white or brightly colored flowers with simple petal arrangements, such as small orchids, roses, sweet peas, or violets.

1 egg white
Flowers
Superfine sugar

1. Place egg white in a small bowl and stir lightly.
2. Dip flowers, one at a time, in egg white or apply egg white with a fine artist's brush; cover all parts.
3. Remove excess white to prevent petals from sticking together.
4. Sprinkle sugar over petals, covering all egg white, and shaking to avoid clumping. Blow softly on flowers to remove excess sugar.
5. Place flowers on aluminum foil-lined baking sheet. Allow to dry in a cool place for 2 to 3 days.

Above right: An edible starburst of asparagus spears radiates around a wreath of scallops and watercress.
Right: An unusual decoration for fish is slices of kiwifruit topped by tomato roses.

Christmas Cookies

Wherever Christmas is celebrated, cooks have created a repertoire of special sweets to honor the season. In some countries cookie-baking starts weeks before Christmas. Dried and candied fruits, nuts, spices, and pounds of butter fill the larder, to be turned into wreaths, rings, bars, stars, and—of course—gingerbread.

Gingerbread People

It wouldn't be Christmas without these little cookie people, thickly cut from a spicy molasses dough.

*½ cup unsalted butter,
  softened*
½ cup firmly packed brown sugar
½ cup molasses
1 egg
2½ cups flour
1 teaspoon baking soda
½ teaspoon salt
2 teaspoons ground ginger
1 teaspoon ground cinnamon
½ teaspoon ground nutmeg
½ teaspoon ground cloves
Dried currants, for decorating

1. In large mixer bowl cream butter; gradually add sugar and beat until light. Add molasses and egg and beat to blend well; set aside.
2. In a bowl stir together flour, baking soda, salt, ginger, cinnamon, nutmeg, and cloves. Gradually add flour mixture to butter mixture, beating until just blended. Gather dough into a ball and refrigerate in plastic wrap for at least 1 hour.
3. Preheat oven to 325° F. On a lightly floured board, roll out gingerbread to a thickness of ¼ inch. Cut out cookies and transfer to greased baking sheets. Bake until lightly browned around edges and feel barely firm when touched gently (about 10 minutes). Transfer to wire racks. While cookies are still hot, press in currants to simulate eyes, mouths, and buttons. When cool, decorate with Royal Icing piped from a paper cone (see below).
*Yields approximately 1 dozen
4-inch-long cookies.*

Royal Icing

1¼ cups sifted confectioners' sugar
1 egg white
1 teaspoon strained lemon juice
Food coloring (optional)

In a small bowl combine ¾ cup of the sugar with egg white and lemon juice. Beat until thick and white (about 10 minutes). Add remaining sugar and beat until stiff. If desired, tint icing with food coloring.
Yields ¾ cup.

*Children can be kept amused
for hours
decorating gingerbread
people with a piping cone.*

Making a Paper Piping Cone

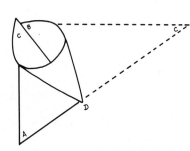

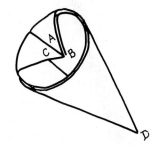

Cut a square of parchment paper in half diagonally. (Use only one of the triangles.) Take the right-hand point (C) and fold it in toward the middle point (B). Then take the opposite point (A) and fold it around until it also meets the middle point (B) at the top.

The three points now meet to form a closed tip (D). Fold the point at the open end of the cone over toward the closed tip of the cone to prevent the cone from unraveling.

To use the cone, fill it no more than half full. Fold the open end of the piping cone down toward the filling. Cut the closed end of the cone with scissors to form an opening that will fit the size of the icing tip to be used.

Cinnamon Stars

Crunchy German *Zimtsterne* (cinnamon stars) contain no flour or fat. They are meringue based, stiffened with ground almonds. Sticky dough is easier to pat out than to roll.

3 egg whites, at room temperature
Pinch salt
1¼ cups superfine sugar
1 tablespoon ground cinnamon
5 to 5½ cups finely ground
*   unblanched almonds*

1. In mixer bowl beat egg whites with salt to soft peaks. Gradually add sugar; beat at high speed 10 minutes. With a spoon remove ¾ cup of the meringue and set aside. Using lowest speed, add cinnamon to remaining meringue and beat thoroughly.
2. Add 4½ cups of the ground almonds to meringue, folding them in gently but thoroughly.
3. Pat out dough to a thickness of about ¼ inch. To prevent dough from sticking, sprinkle work surface with the remaining ½ to 1 cup ground almonds (use as much as needed). Cut dough with a star-shaped cutter. Transfer cookies to greased and floured baking sheets.
4. Using a pastry brush or table knife, paint top of each cookie with an even layer of reserved meringue. Let cookies stand in a cool place for 2 hours.
5. Preheat oven to 300° F. Bake until cookies are very lightly colored and tops feel firm when touched gently (about 20 minutes). Cool 5 minutes on baking sheets, then transfer to wire racks to cool completely. Store in an airtight container.
Yields about 2 dozen 3-inch cookies.

Scottish Yule Bannock

To distinguish Christmas shortbread from the kind made the year around, some Scottish bakers add minced almonds and candied citron. This Yule bannock (bread) is cut into bite-sized cubes after baking.

1½ cups flour
¼ teaspoon salt
⅜ cup confectioners' sugar
⅓ cup finely minced, candied
*   citron or mixed candied fruit*
¼ cup finely minced, toasted
*   almonds*
¾ cup unsalted butter, cut into
*   pieces and slightly softened*
1½ tablespoons granulated sugar

1. Preheat oven to 325° F.
2. To prepare in a food processor: In work bowl of food processor, combine flour, salt, and confectioners' sugar. Pulse briefly until just blended. Add citron, almonds, and butter. Pulse several times until mixture resembles fine crumbs.
To prepare by hand: On a cool work surface, combine flour, salt, and sugar; stir to blend. Add citron and almonds; toss to coat citron with flour mixture. Cut in butter with pastry blender or 2 knives until mixture resembles fine crumbs.
3. Lightly press dough into an 8-inch-square baking pan, then sprinkle with granulated sugar. Bake until lightly browned (about 30 minutes). Immediately cut into 64 squares. Let cool in pan 10 minutes, then transfer to a wire rack to finish cooling.
Yields 64 cookies.

As the name implies,
Zimtsterne cookies, above,
are traditionally
baked in the shape of stars.

Pudding & Pie

Traditionally, Christmas dinners in England were extraordinarily lavish and excessive feasts. It is hard to believe, but one medieval menu called for 17 main dishes, including roast boar, beef tongue, pig, goose, swan, turkey, boiled capon and beef, roast beef, venison, lamb, mince pie, and olive pie! An account in the *Newcastle Chronicle* enumerated the ingredients of an impressive Christmas pie: 20 pounds butter, 2 bushels flour, 4 geese, 4 wild ducks, 2 rabbits, 2 woodcocks, 2 turkeys, 6 snipes, 4 partridge, 2 tongues, 7 blackbirds, and 6 pigeons. Measuring 9 feet in diameter and weighing 12 stone (1 stone is the equivalent of 14 pounds), the pie needed two men to carry it to the table.

In England the term pudding describes a dish—not necessarily a dessert—with a cereal base, often containing lard or suet and boiled in a cloth bag. One of the earliest puddings, predating the 1700s, was called frumenty or furmety. To make this dish, wheat was boiled until the grains burst. When cooled it was strained and boiled again in broth or in milk and egg yolks. The result was served as an accompaniment to venison or mutton. It was not until later that raisins, sugar, and spices were added, giving it a sweeter taste.

Early frumenty is probably a forerunner of that peculiarly English plum pudding and

plum porridge. One of the first recorded mentions of the plum pudding was in a tract of the early 1700s called "Round About Our Coal Fire": "In Christmas holidays the tables were all spread from the first to the last; the sirloins of beef, the minced pies, the plum porridge, the capons, geese, turkeys, and plum puddings were all brought upon the board." A simple recipe for plum pudding of the time listed the ingredients as beef or mutton broth combined with brown bread, raisins, currants, dried plums (prunes), mace, and gingerbread. The finished product was semiliquid rather than a solid shape.

As the recipe evolved, plums were eliminated from the list of ingredients but the name remains, probably because the ingredients include other dried fruit, usually raisins. A 1791 recipe listed the ingredients in plum pudding as raisins, candied fruit, figs, beef suet, bread crumbs, flour, cinnnamon, brown sugar, cloves, cider or fruit juice, sherry flavoring, and eggs. The *Daily Telegraph* of January 21, 1890, recommended the following method: "The cook is to take dough, beer in the course of fermentation, milk, brandy, whiskey, and gin in equal parts; bread, citronate, large and small raisins in profusion. This must be stirred by the whole family for at least three days, and it is then to be hung up in a linen bag for six weeks in order thoroughly to ferment."

There is little doubt about the popularity of plum pudding. An account tells of a dish brought to the Paighton Fair near Exeter: Composed of 400 pounds of flour, 170 pounds of beef suet, 140 pounds of raisins, and 240 eggs, the pudding was boiled for 4 days and weighed 800 pounds when cooked. It was taken through the streets and handed out to the poor.

Many puddings of more modest proportion became popular in England during the eighteenth-century. But it was the plum pudding that came to be the Christmas favorite and this was what early English settlers brought to America.

Gumdrop Eaves & Wafer Shingles

Bakers young and old are enchanted by the magic of a gingerbread house. Use it on the table or under the tree. Carefully cut and assembled, this one will keep for years if it is stored in a cool, dry place.

Three cakes are needed to make this house and each one should be baked separately. Do not triple the recipe; it is difficult to handle such a large quantity of dough. Bake cakes at least a day before assembling the house—they will be firmer and easier to work with.

Royal Icing is the edible glue that holds the pieces of the house together and sticks the candy decorations to the walls and roof. Icing also outlines the windows and doors. Because it is fast-drying, the icing is best made in three

batches and used quickly, before it forms a crust and clogs the tip in the pastry bag.

The roof of the house is tiled with 13 to 16 ounces of multicolored wafers; the eaves, door and window frames, and foundations are trimmed with 10 ounces of spice-flavored gumdrops, 8 ounces of oval candy disks, 6 ounces of bear-shaped jellied candies, 10 peppermint sticks, and 16 ounces of sliced candy sticks.

7½ cups sifted flour
1½ teaspoons baking soda
1 teaspoon salt
1 tablespoon ground cinnamon
2 teaspoons ground ginger
1 teaspoon each ground nutmeg and ground cloves
1½ cups vegetable shortening
1½ cups sugar
12 ounces light molasses
1 tablespoon vanilla extract
1 tablespoon grated orange rind
Candies, for decorating
4½ cups Royal Icing

1. In a small bowl combine 1½ cups of the flour, baking soda, salt, cinnamon, ginger, nutmeg, and cloves; stir until thoroughly blended.

2. Preheat oven to 325° F. Combine shortening and sugar in another mixing bowl and beat until fluffy and well blended. Beat in molasses, vanilla, and orange rind. Gradually add flour mixture, beating until well combined. Add remaining 6 cups flour, 1 cup at a time, mixing until well blended. When dough stiffens, knead until smooth.

3. Place dough in a greased, lightly floured, shallow-rimmed, 10½- by 15½-inch baking pan. Pat dough into pan with your fingers; smooth it out with a rolling pin.

4. Bake gingerbread until it pulls away from sides of pan and feels firm to the touch (about 35 minutes). Cool in pan on a wire rack for 5 minutes. While still warm, cut out Gingerbread House pieces as described in Assembly.
Yields 1 cake. (3 cakes needed for Gingerbread House. Mix and bake these one at a time.)

Royal Icing

2 egg whites
3½ cups confectioners' sugar

In a small bowl beat egg whites with electric mixer until stiff. Add sugar, ½ cup at a time, beating to incorporate completely after each addition. Continue beating at high speed until icing is very stiff (about 5 minutes).
Yields about 1½ cups icing (3 batches needed to make House).

Making Patterns

1. Make a grid of 1-inch squares on stiff cardboard. Draw patterns for all pieces, then cut them out. (Refer to drawings for measurements.)

2. Without removing gingerbread from pan, place patterns and cut 2 roof pieces within the edges of 1 still-warm cake. From second cake cut 1 end wall and 2 chimney segments. From third cake, cut second end wall, side walls, 4 wall posts, and 1 chimney segment. Leave cut gingerbread in pan until completely cool.

Assembly

1. When completely cool, lift pieces out of the pans. Set them on flat working surface.

2. Prepare 1 batch of Royal Icing. Decorate all 4 walls piping on 1 row of icing at a time and pressing candy decorations into it. Allow icing to dry (about 15 minutes).

3. Place gingerbread base onto a board or tray.

4. Prepare second batch of icing. On 1 end and 1 side wall, pipe icing onto all edges except the roofline; press together to form corner and set walls onto base. Hold in place a few minutes until set. Repeat with other end and side wall. Allow icing to dry. Pipe icing into inside corners; press wall posts into place. Let walls stand undisturbed until icing is completely dry (at least 3 hours, or overnight).

5. Prepare third batch of icing. Pipe icing onto one face of each chimney segment; then stick segments together into a 3-decker sandwich. Pipe icing onto bottom of assembled chimney; set on one roof piece. Decorate both roof pieces before assembling them with a line of icing along eaves; press in candy wafers. Repeat rows of icing and wafers until roof is covered.

6. Pipe icing onto top edges of walls. Position 1 roof piece. Hold in place until set. Repeat with other roof piece. Pipe icing along the peak.

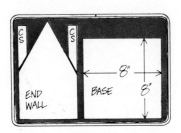

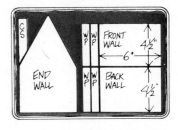

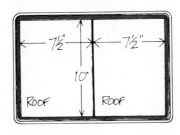

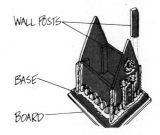

CHAPTER 7

Gifts Of Love

Pretty wrappings and personal greetings are introduced by Santa

The old adage that "it is better to give than to receive" is never more true than at Christmas. The spirit of "goodwill to all men" is in the air, rung out by church bells, signaled by twinkling lights, and sung by carollers.

In keeping with this spirit, you will not find the answer to your problem of what to give Uncle John. This chapter does not contain handy shopping lists. What it does give you is some wrapping ideas for presenting your gifts and some scents that can be part of your Christmas decorations and, in a pinch, be wrapped as gifts. See From My Kitchen to Yours on page 149 for homemade food that can also save a last-minute dash to crowded stores.

Who can fail to be charmed by Santa—whatever you call him and whether you believe in him or not. The section that follows covers the history and lore that surrounds this depiction of the Christmas season.

If you are interested in how traditions start, read Old-fashioned Greetings that starts on page 180. You might be surprised by some of the interesting facts relating to printed greeting cards.

Santa has many guises. He appears in Victorian decals that can be pasted onto packages, preceding pages, and is known to delight a little girl whether she is painted, opposite page, or sitting on his knee, left.

Boxing Day

On first hearing it, the term Boxing Day might seem to refer to the commemoration of a well-known sport, rather than to the English tradition of giving presents on the day after Christmas.

Christmas gift-giving customs have shown remarkable variety throughout the world since presents were first given at the holidays in ancient times. In some countries presents are exchanged and opened on Christmas Eve. In North America the custom is to place gifts under the tree on Christmas Eve and open them on Christmas Day. In England, Australia, and Canada, gifts are presented to servants, tradesmen, and other service workers on December 26— Boxing Day.

Boxing Day originated, in practice if not in name, nearly 500 years ago. In the Middle Ages each church kept an alms box in which parishioners placed donations throughout the year. The box was opened on December 26 and its contents distributed to the poor.

The custom gradually became secularized. Adapting the practices of the church, apprentices and servants began to keep their own boxes. Made in early times of earthenware, these boxes held savings and donations from customers, patrons, and friends. Like alms boxes, the containers were opened on December 26 and the money was counted. To break the box open early was to invite bad luck.

In England, presents came to be given on Boxing Day to lamplighters, waits (watch-men), parish workers, and other people in the community who performed regular services throughout the year. The custom, which continues to be celebrated in England on December 26, was transported to America, where presents are given at the holidays to mail carriers, gardeners, and other people who provide ongoing services to a household.

In Holland and parts of Germany, children save pennies in earthenware boxes formed in the shape of a pig and break them open at Christmas. The container was called a "feast pig," and represents an early version of our modern piggy bank.

All Wrapped Up

I n the same way that food tastes better when it is beautifully arranged and garnished, presents are enjoyed more when they are artfully wrapped. Even a token gift becomes special when it is presented in an attractive package.

If you do your Christmas shopping early, you can get around the problem by having gifts wrapped by the stores at which you make your purchases. However, once the rush begins, the gift-wrap lines get long. Also, your choices of paper and bows are limited to ones that the stores consider suitable, so you may lose the opportunity to make the presentation as appropriate as the gift.

It is recommended that you always ask for a suitably sized box to accompany your purchase—the only difficult part of wrapping is trying to make a neat package out of an oddball shape. Armed with a boxed gift, the rest is pure fun.

Outer Covers

Stores are full of patterned papers and brightly colored bows and ties. But there are many alternatives if you have a little imagination and want your gift to appear special.

Instead of paper, use fabric. This is particularly appropriate when wrapping a gift for a friend who likes to sew. If you tie the package with a generous amount of rickrack or lace trim, the wrapping will be as much of a gift as the contents.

Other ideas for making the outer covering part of the gift are folding bars of soap into hand towels or wrapping a gift of china in pretty dish towels. The box containing a shirt for a male friend can be tied with a belt or a necktie; the one containing a dress for a young girl can be tied with matching hair ribbons.

Leftover wallcovering makes good, strong wrapping paper. Or, if you don't have scraps, purchase a full roll or a discontinued book of samples.

Sheets of newspaper can reflect the gift receiver's personality or interests. Use the financial pages for your stockbroker friends, the real estate section for a newly engaged couple, or the *London Times* for the child who received a trip to England as a graduation gift.

Crepe paper is especially good for wrapping gifts that just won't fit into a square box. It is strong and it stretches around curves. Use just one color or wrap the gift in several, different-colored sheets. Fold back a portion of each successive layer for a rainbow effect.

Ties

As well as the more usual pieces of ribbon, there are numerous materials that hold wrapping in place. Lace and rickrack as well as belts and ties have already been mentioned. Following are a few more ideas.

For a large gift you can use lengths of good-looking rope from a boating-supply store; heavy twine can also be attractive as well as sturdy.

For small gifts, snap a ponytail band around the wrapped box or use attractive pieces of trim salvaged from the remnants counter in the notions department. Or, clean out your sewing materials closet and tear strips of fabric on the bias and stitch them together to make long lengths. Crochet scraps of wool into chains.

A jewelry box also usually yields some interesting ties. Strands of beads that are no longer worn add

sparkle to a small gift. If you don't want to part with any of your own necklaces, thrift shops often have boxes full of junk jewelry that is priced very reasonably.

Finishing Touches

Now that your gift is wrapped prettily and tied with flair, it is ready to give. But for an extra touch, why not add a little decoration? Bells, sprigs of holly, a small tree ornament, and decals are all embellishments that will give the recipient pleasure.

Most places that sell gift-wrapping materials also offer printed gift tags. For more unusual decorations, check out a well-stocked office-supply or stationery store. They sell bundles of price tags in bright colors that make economical gift tags. You can find the large, gold and silver, foil decals used as corporate seals, which make attractive decorations, colorful file folder labels, stock certificate blanks, and address labels.

Similar-shaped boxes appear very different when they are wrapped with thought. These photographs show how you can present gifts that are appropriate for the contents and for the recipients.

177

Color Me Red

To make your own decals or stencils to decorate cards, gift tags, and wrapping paper, try using some of these old-fashioned ornaments. Trace or copy on a duplicating machine, cut them out, and color them.

A tussie mussie is a sweet-smelling nosegay used in Victorian times to overpower objectionable odors.

Half-Century Potpourri

Potpourris used to be made by the moist method in which herbs are salted down in a crock, then mixed with spices, oils, a fixative, and a dash of brandy or perfume. The fragrances last for many years.

Here's one recipe for moist potpourri you can use as a guide for creating your own. It's called Half-Century Potpourri because it's said that it will keep its fragrance for up to 50 years, with the addition of a bit of brandy every couple of years or whenever the mixture dries out.

¾ cup salt (noniodized)
3 bay leaves, crushed
¼ cup allspice, crushed
¼ cup cloves, crushed
¼ cup brown sugar
1 tablespoon orrisroot powder
1 quart partially dried rose petals, preferably old species
2 cups mixed, partially dried fragrant garden flowers (jasmine, lavender, orange blossoms, violets, etc.)
1 cup dried fragrant leaves (rose geranium, bee balm, lemon verbena, etc.)
2 tablespoons brandy

1. Mix together salt, bay, allspice, cloves, and sugar. Set aside.
2. Blend flower petals and leaves with orrisroot. Place some of the petal mixture in a large crock and sprinkle with the salt mixture. Continue alternating layers of petals and salt, ending with salt. Add brandy, weight down layered petals with a plate, and seal tightly.
3. Let stand for one month, stirring every day. At the end of the month, stir the mixture thoroughly and pour into small containers.

Sachets

Sachets are little bags or envelopes filled with dried potpourri that are ideal to give as Christmas gifts. Traditionally, they are added to clothes drawers, linen closets, sweater boxes, or anywhere you want to have a fresh clean scent.

To make old-fashioned sachets, wrap potpourri inside pretty handkerchiefs or squares of lace or very thin fabric and tie into little balls or fold into interesting shapes. Trim with bits of lace and ribbons or maybe a dried flower.

For sachets that will repel moths, stuff with southernwood, wormwood, thyme, lavendar, santolina, or tansy. Lay or tie the bags around winter garments in storage.

If you want a pillow for napping, make a large envelope of a soft fabric and stuff part of it or a quilted section or an applique with the potpourri. If you have lots of herbs, stuff the whole pillow. Herbal pillows are great gifts for people confined to bed.

When you make sachets, don't forget the cats. Stuff dried catnip leaves into a sachet to please your own pets or those of your friends.

Tussie Mussies

The Elizabethans carried little nosegays of fresh herbs and flowers, known as tussie mussies, to overpower objectionable odors. It became the custom to present the little bouquets in silvered water tubes as personal expressions of sentiments. Different plants held special meanings in the language of flowers.

Today the little herbal bouquets are sometimes carried by brides or given on special days. Made from fresh or dried herbal materials, tussie mussies can also be used as decorative potpourris for tabletops or displayed in little vases.

Start with a circle or border of scented leaves such as rose geranium.

Add sprigs of herbs to fill the center, accent with flowers, and tie it all together with a piece of ribbon. Add a collar of lace if you like.

Make the bouquet from fresh materials and let it dry naturally in a warm dry place. Or start with dried sprigs of herbs and flowers wired to some fresh stems. Sprinkle with a bit of orrisroot or other potpourri fixative and add a few drops of fragrant oils to preserve the natural scents.

Scenting the Air

Before Christmas, the aromas of baking bread and cookies often waft through the house. But, by the time Christmas has come and the guests have arrived, the kitchen has been cleaned and those wonderful smells have disappeared. Following are ways to add nose-tingling excitement to the festivities.

Throw cinnamon sticks, whole cloves, whole allspice, a lemon, an orange, and maybe some apple peelings into a saucepan full of water. Bring water to the boil, then simmer. It won't be long before the house is filled with a spicy aroma.

Add a special aroma to the smell of an open fire by burning cedar, pine, and juniper incense or chips along with the logs.

Drip perfumed oils and essences, available at soap stores, onto unglazed terra-cotta tiles or bowls. They will absorb the liquid and release the scent back into the room gradually. You can also put drops of perfume onto light bulbs. When the fixture is on, the hot air generated by the lit bulb will scent the entire room.

Top: Grapevine chips scent the smoke from an open fire. Above: The aroma of simmering fruit and spices will waft through the house.

Pomander Balls

Old-fashioned pomander balls are simply fruits studded with whole cloves, then dried. These natural air fresheners are as decorative as they are practical. They can be added to a Christmas punch, hung in the closet to repel moths, used as tree ornaments and place-card holders, stacked in a bowl as a centerpiece, or given away as gifts.

In order to make good-looking pomander balls, select perfect pieces of fruit. Oranges are the most popular, but apples, grapefruit, lemons, limes, pears, even kumquats can be used to make balls of various shapes and sizes.

Tradition calls for studding the fruit all over closely with whole cloves. As the fruit dries, the skin shrinks and draws the cloves closer together. Today, many people who make pomanders prefer to save time and add the cloves in rows or patterns or scatter them over the surface leaving some of the fruit skin showing. These areas can be left plain when dried or decorated with small dried flowers or sprigs of herbs or seed head. Always buy good-quality whole cloves that are strongly scented.

Traditionally, the clove-studded fruit is rolled in the ingredients mentioned below.

Perfectly formed oranges or other kinds of fruit
Fresh, high-quality whole cloves
Orrisroot, nutmeg, cinnamon, allspice, cardamom, musk (These are the spices traditionally used. Add or substitute others as desired.)

1. Stud the surface of each orange with cloves. Traditionally, the entire surface is densely and evenly covered. Making rows and patterns is an attractive variation. A more elaborate variation calls for

substituting sprigs of herbs or dried flowers for cloves in some areas of the orange.

To make the task easier and quicker and to avoid breaking cloves (and fingernails), hold the fruit in one hand and make a tiny hole in the skin with a nail, skewer, or any handy sharp instrument. Press a clove all the way into the hole with your finger. Finish studding the day you start, before the fruit starts to dry.

2. Roll orange in one or more of the ground spices listed.

3. If you plan to hang the pomander, insert a skewer, knitting needle, or straight piece of clothes-hanger wire completely through the fruit. As it dries, turn the fruit on the wire regularly to keep it from sticking.

4. To dry studded orange, place in a sunny warm, dry spot for 1 to 2 weeks. Turn studded orange periodically so it will dry evenly.

If you're in a big hurry, sit the pomander on a baking sheet and put it in a gas oven with a pilot light. Do not turn on the heat. Leave oven door ajar until the fruit has dried.

5. When the orange has dried, use a crochet hook to draw ribbon, yarn, or cord through the hole. To prevent the pomander from slipping off, tie one end into a bow or knot, or thread on a bead. If you prefer, sew a tassel onto the end of the ribbon.

SPECIAL THANKS TO

Lauren Adams and Alice Erb,
The Tail of the Yak Trading
Company, Berkeley, Calif.
Kurt S. Adler, Inc., New York
Americian Pie, San Francisco
American Tree Co., New York
Bronson Imports, New York
Mrs. Pierce B. Browne
A.T. Brugger, Piedmont, Calif.
Greg and Kathy Calegari,
San Francisco
California Christmas Tree Growers,
Lafayette, Calif.
Guy Chaddock & Co. Showrooms,
San Francisco
Churchill Enterprises,
San Bruno, Calif.
Rick Cliff
Barbara Colvin, San Francisco
Tom Courtright, Orchard Nursery,
Lafayette, Calif.
Dandelion, San Francisco
Jeffrey Davies, San Francisco
Tom Downs, Pasack Sales,
Mahwah, N.J.
Aaron and Shirley Ferer,
Hillsborough, Calif.
Carl Ernitz and Linda Gatto,
San Francisco
Barbara Belloli and Jean Thompson,
Fiondella, San Francisco
Mr and Mrs Harvey Freedman,
Piedmont, Calif.
Garden Study Club of the Peninsula

Mr and Mrs Gatto, San Francisco
General Electric Co., Cleveland
Gilbert Mfg., Long Island City, N.Y.
Good Tidings, Linthicum
Heights, Md.
Dolph Gotelli, Sacramento, Calif.
Helen Gregory, San Rafael, Calif.
GTE Products, Burlingame, Calif.
Harvest, Corrales, N. Mex.
Muriel Herbert,
Muriel Herbert Interiors,
Piedmont, Calif.
Betty Hoyt, Bodega Bay, Calif.
Seymour L. Jeruss, Noma
International, Forest Park, Ill.
Sue Fisher King, San Francisco
Leco Electric Mfg Co., Dallas
Manheim Galleries, San Francisco
Marian May, San Francisco
Rex May, The Christmas Store,
San Francisco
David and Linda McFadden
C. L. McRae, San Francisco
Mexican Museum, San Francisco
Holly Money, AIFD, San Francisco
Ron Morgan
Ron Morgan Floral Design,
Piedmont, Calif.
Robert Mueller, Berkeley, Calif.
National Christmas Tree Assoc.,
Milwaukee, Wis.
National Ornament & Electric Lights
Christmas Assoc., New York
The Original Christmas Store,
San Francisco

Tim Oates, San Francisco
Orchard Nursery and Florist,
Lafayette, Calif.
Gwen Perrin, Mill Valley, Calif.
Mr and Mrs Richard Pogue,
Piedmont, Calif.
Liz Pratt, Orinda, Calif.
Greg Renfrow, Benicia, Calif.
Jim Roberts, Santa Rose, Calif.
Sacramento Street Christmas Store,
San Francisco
Mr and Mrs Charles Saunders,
William and Josephine Sommers,
Hillsborough, Calif.
Susan Tankersley, Wisteria,
Berkeley, Calif.
Charles Thompson, San Francisco
John Tilford, Western Garden
Nursery, Hayward, Calif.
Sirpa Tuomainen and Robert
Hourula, Berkeley, Calif.
Dan Upchurch, AAF, AIFD,
Ribbon Narrow World Wide,
Secaucus, N.J.
Henry Wangeman, Tzintzuntzan,
Berkeley, Calif.
Mary Lou Weggenman, Children's
Hospital Branches, Oakland, Calif.
Carol Ann Prezel, West Portal Floral
Co., San Francisco
Western Garden Nursery,
Hayward, Calif.
Wildwood Holiday Home Tour,
Piedmont, Calif.
Yoko's, San Francisco

INDEX